THE LAW OF PRIVACY AND THE MEDIA

FIRST CUMULATIVE UPDATING SUPPLEMENT

THE LAW OF
PRIVACY
AND THE
MEDIA

FIRST CUMULATIVE
UPDATING SUPPLEMENT

Edited by
SIR MICHAEL TUGENDHAT
Judge of the High Court of England and Wales

IAIN CHRISTIE
*Barrister, formerly Assistant Legal Adviser to the Foreign and
Commonwealth Office*

FIVE RAYMOND BUILDINGS

OXFORD
UNIVERSITY PRESS

OXFORD

UNIVERSITY PRESS

Great Clarendon Street, Oxford OX2 6DP

Oxford University Press is a department of the University of Oxford.
It furthers the University's objective of excellence in research, scholarship,
and education by publishing worldwide in

Oxford New York

Auckland Bangkok Buenos Aires Cape Town Chennai
Dar es Salaam Delhi Hong Kong Istanbul Karachi Kolkata
Kuala Lumpur Madrid Melbourne Mexico City Mumbai Nairobi
São Paulo Shanghai Taipei Tokyo Toronto

Oxford is a registered trade mark of Oxford University Press
in the UK and in certain other countries

Published in the United States
by Oxford University Press Inc., New York

British Library Cataloguing in Publication Data

Data available

Library of Congress Cataloging in Publication Data

Data available

ISBN 0–19–926878–9 (Supplement)
ISBN 0–19–926879–7 (Main Work plus Supplement)

1 3 5 7 9 10 8 6 4 2

Typeset by Cambrian Typesetters, Frimley, Surrey

Printed in Great Britain
on acid-free paper by
Ashford Colour Press Limited, Gosport, Hampshire

EDITORS

Sir Michael Tugendhat

Iain Christie

CONTRIBUTORS

Desmond Browne QC

Adrienne Page QC

James Price QC

Richard Parkes QC

Mark Warby QC

Stephen Bate

Andrew Monson

Alexandra Marzec

Tony Smith

David Sherborne

Justin Rushbrooke

Matthew Nicklin

Jonathan Barnes

Godwin Busuttil

Adam Wolanski

William Bennett

Christina Michalos

Jacob Dean

Anna Coppola

Sara Mansoori

Adam Speker

Sapna Jethani

FIVE RAYMOND BUILDINGS

CONTENTS—SUMMARY

VI ISSUES OF SPECIAL INTEREST TO THE MEDIA

TABLES OF CASES

United Kingdom

European Commission and Court of Human Rights

European Court of Justice

Foreign

Australia

Austria

Canada

France

Germany

Ireland

The Netherlands

New Zealand

South Africa

USA

TABLES OF ADJUDICATIONS OF THE MEDIA REGULATORS

Broadcasting Standards Commission

Press Complaints Commission

TABLES OF LEGISLATION

UK Statutory Instruments

TABLE OF TREATIES, CONVENTIONS, AND OTHER INTERNATIONAL INSTRUMENTS

1

CONTEXT AND BACKGROUND

A. Introduction

The House of Lords upheld the decision of the Court of Appeal in *Wainwright v*   **1.01**
Home Office [2003] 3 WLR 1137 dismissing the Claimants' claim for damages occasioned by strip searches in breach of the procedure laid down under the Prison Rules. Their Lordships confirmed that English law does not recognise a general tort of invasion of privacy. Some gaps in the existing law could be filled by judicious development of an existing principle [18], others only by legislation. The Human Rights Act 1998 was itself a substantial gap-filler: [33]–[34]. They left open for another day, however, the question whether, in relation to publication of personal information obtained by intrusion, certain actions for breach of confidence might be renamed invasions of privacy: [28]–[30].

B. Common Law and Equity

(1) Trespass and Wrongful Interference with Goods

1.03   Substantial damages have been given for trespass in the Queensland case of *Grosse v Purvis* [2003] QDC 151 noted in the Supplement to paras 11.35 and 11.46 below.

1.05   In *Wainwright v Home Office* [2003] 3 WLR 1137 Lord Hoffmann expressed complete agreement with Buxton LJ's remarks at [2002] QB 1334 [67]–[72] that *Wilkinson v Downton* has nothing to do with trespass to the person.

(2) Nuisance

1.06   Substantial damages have been given for nuisance in the Queensland case of *Grosse v Purvis* [2003] QDC 151 noted in the Supplement to paras 11.35 and 11.46 below.

(3) Breach of Confidence

1.08   n20 In *Campbell v MGN Ltd* [2003] QB 658 at [70] the Court of Appeal observed that unjustifiable disclosure of information relating to an aspect of an individual's private life which he does not choose to make public would be better described as breach of privacy rather than breach of confidence. This observation was not specifically referred to by the House of Lords in *Wainwright v Home Office* but is consistent with Lord Hoffmann's interpretation of Sedley LJ's remarks in *Douglas v Hello! Ltd* [2001] QB 967 [125]–[126].

1.09   n23 In *A v B plc* [2003] QB 195 at [11](ix) the Court of Appeal held that 'the need for a confidential relationship should not give rise to problems as to the law. A duty of confidence will arise whenever the party subject to the duty is in a situation where he either knows or ought to know that the other person can reasonably expect his privacy to be protected.'

C. Legislation

(3) The Data Protection Act 1998

1.20   n49 In *Campbell v MGN Ltd* at [97]–[107] the Court of Appeal confirmed that the Data Protection Act 1998 does apply to the media's dealings with information. See further the Supplement to para 5.25 below.

1.21   n52 The awards made by Morland J were set aside by the Court of Appeal which found that the defendant had made out a good defence under s 32 of the Data Protection Act, which applied both pre and post publication. See further the Supplement to para 5.80 below.

(5) Other legislation

(a) Newsgathering from public bodies and officials

n73 The House of Lords' decision in *R v Shayler* is now reported at [2003] 1 AC   **1.24**
247.

(f) Reports of crime and the courts

n90 In November 2002 the House of Commons Home Affairs Select Committee   **1.29**
recommended that consideration be given to the grant of anonymity to those accused of sex crimes: Home Affairs Committee Second Report 2002–2003, 28
November 2002, HC 83, para 145. The Home Office was unconvinced: see its
Response of March 2003 Cm 5787, para (gg).

(g) Privacy of journalistic material

n103 Journalistic material is subject to certain qualified exemptions and excep-   **1.30**
tions from the access rights under the Data Protection Act 1998 and, where this is
otherwise applicable, the Freedom of Information Act 2000: Data Protection Act
1998, s 32. See paras 5.79–5.86 of the Main Work and the Supplement thereto.
The Freedom of Information Act 2000 applies in qualified form to the BBC,
Channel Four, and S4C: see para 1.22 of the Main Work. Where the access rights
do apply, the identities of sources may be withheld if they do not consent and it is
'reasonable' to withhold their identities: Data Protection Act 1998, s 7(4). See
Main Work paras 5.56–5.57.

The Terrorism Act 2000 has been amended to add a further criminal offence of   **1.31**
failing without reasonable excuse to disclose information which a person knows
or believes might be of material assistance in preventing an act of terrorism or in
securing the apprehension, prosecution or conviction of a person for terrorist acts:
s 38B, inserted by s 117 of the Anti-Terrorism, Crime and Security Act 2001.
Unlike the offence under s 19 of the Act of 2000, this new crime is not limited to
information obtained in the course of employment.

D. Reviews and Reform

The following new paragraphs come at the end of Section D:

(8) Report into Media and Press Intrusion 2003

In June 2002, after hearing eight days of oral evidence, the Department of Culture   **1.62A**
Media and Sport Select Committee published its Report into Media and Press
Intrusion: 5th Report of Session 2002–2003 HC 458-1. The report came at a

time of growing calls for some form of statutory regulation of the press. During the reading of the Communications Bill, veteran backbenchers Chris Mullin and Clive Soley had proposed amendments which would give the new media regulator Ofcom greater power over the content of the press. In March 2003 Ministers ruled out statutory regulation of the press at the third reading of the Bill in the House of Commons, the final stage before it moved to the House of Lords, where a number of peers believed there should be tighter restrictions on the press. Lord McNally, a Liberal Democrat peer, made a further attempt to introduce an amendment to the Communications Bill giving Ofcom wide powers over the PCC, and in particular the power to impose penalties of up to £500,000 on newspapers which breach the PCC code. The Government vowed to whip Labour peers into the lobbies to reject any move to bring the PCC under Ofcom.

1.62B   Publication of the Report also coincided with widespread condemnation of the PCC for its apparent inability to provide a sufficient remedy for the invasion of privacy suffered by the DJ Sara Cox and her husband. *The People*—the editor of which was a Commission member—had published long lens photographs of the couple nude on a beach during their honeymoon. An immediate complaint was made to the PCC, which arranged publication of a prominent apology, but Ms Cox and her husband went on to sue the paper and secure a settlement reported to total £50,000 in damages plus some £200,000 in legal costs. The case was interpreted by many as illustrating the toothlessness of the PCC as well as the apparent anomaly of having as a Commission member the editor of a flagrantly offending publication. The PCC vehemently rejected these criticisms, stating that it had been precluded from adjudicating on the case because Ms Cox had brought legal proceedings.

1.62C   During the Committee's hearings, tabloid editors were met with hostility by some MPs. Against this background it came as a surprise to many that the conclusions of the Committee regarding press standards were generally positive. The Committee expressed the view that, overall, standards of press behaviour had improved over the last decade, although it condemned certain press practices, such as doorstepping of people who have refused to be interviewed, and media scrums, approving Lord Wakeham's description of them as a form of collective harassment.

1.62D   The Committee also expressed the view in its report that the performance of the PCC—which it described as 'slightly too softly softly'—had improved in the last decade. However, shortly after publication of the Report, Chris Bryant MP, a member of the Committee, remarked that the PCC had failed to convince the Committee that it was serious about improving standards, and that if the PCC had been more robust in dealing with recent cases—such as the collapse of the Victoria Beckham kidnap trial, in which the key informant had been paid by the

News of the World—the Committee might not have found the need for a privacy law so pressing.

The Committee made several recommendations for improvements to the PCC. **1.62E** These included:

(1) Structural changes to the PCC: the lay majority should be increased, and there should be a more transparent process for appointing lay members of the PCC; press members who preside over persistently offending publications should be required to stand down; there should be lay representation on the Code Committee, which drafts the PCC Code.

(2) The PCC should establish a pre-publication team. This would work to achieve a more consistent approach to foreseeable events that herald intense media activity and people in grief and shock. It would handle enquiries from the public and liaise with the relevant editor. The team would also handle issues related to media harassment and the transmission of 'desist messages' from those who do not want to talk to the media.

(3) The PCC should consider establishing a twin track complaints procedure. The new track would be for complainants who did not want mediation but only wanted the PCC to make a judgment on the code in their case.

(4) Changes to the PCC code, such as the introduction of a ban on payments to the police and a ban on the use and payment of intermediaries such as private detectives to obtain private information from private and public sources about individuals.

(5) The introduction of an obligation on publications required to publish a PCC adjudication that they include a prominent reference to the adjudication on the front page.

(6) The introduction of a 'conscience clause' giving journalists the right to refuse to undertake tasks which breach the code.

(7) The PCC should be empowered to make compensatory awards in serious cases on a fixed scale as well as to order payment of costs incurred by the complainant, not including legal costs.

(8) The PCC should review the rule that matters cannot be dealt with 'for which there was a legal remedy available through the courts to the complainant, such as defamation, unless there is a good reason to do so'.

(9) The PCC should publish a league table of judgments each year, exposing the 'worst offenders'.

(10) The PCC should make itself available to give evidence to the select committee at regular intervals.

On the question of a privacy law, the Committee stated in its report: 'We regard **1.62F** the pragmatic arguments against introducing a privacy law to be quite seductive, especially with regard to the question of limited access to the law for people of ordinary means. However, it seems that the right to respect for private life, introduced into English law by the Human Rights Act 1998, has indeed sown the seed of privacy law. If so, the really pragmatic question is whether its growth should be under the care of the courts, on a case-by-case basis, or of the Government and Parliament.'

1.62G It concluded: 'On balance we firmly recommend that the Government reconsider its position and bring forward legislative proposals to clarify the protection that individuals can expect from unwarranted intrusion by anyone—not the press alone—into their private lives. This is necessary fully to satisfy the obligations upon the UK under the European Convention of Human Rights. There should be full and wide consultation but in the end Parliament should be allowed to undertake its proper legislative role.'

1.62H Introducing the report, Gerald Kaufman MP, the chairman of the Committee, commented: 'It was clear to me that if there were not a properly enacted privacy law then the Human Rights Act would create a de facto privacy law decided by judges ad hoc on the basis of individual cases brought to court inevitably by interested parties.' However he insisted the Committee supported the principle of self-regulation and ruled out any possibility of the new media watchdog, Ofcom, being given any powers over the editorial content of newspapers.

1.62I The Government's immediate response was that it had no intention of introducing a privacy law. Tessa Jowell, the Secretary of State for Culture, Media and Sport, reiterated her support for the current system of press self-regulation which she had voiced in evidence to the Committee, and stated 'the government continues to believe a free press is vital in a democracy and that self-regulation is the best regulatory system'. She added that there was 'room for improvement' by the PCC. In supplementary evidence subsequently disclosed by the Committee, Miss Jowell favoured the proposal that PCC adjudications should be subject to an appeals mechanism independent of government and industry but confirmed that the Government had no plans to legislate in the area of privacy and press intrusion.

1.62J On 15 October 2003 the Government published its response to the Select Committee Report (Command Paper Cm 5985). It rejected the Committee's case for a privacy law, arguing that existing legislation is capable of dealing adequately with questions of privacy. Parliament, it said, should only intervene if there are signs that the courts are systematically striking the wrong balance; but it took the view that there are currently no such signs.

1.62K The Government expressed its commitment to self regulation of the press as 'the best possible way' of balancing the 'sometimes conflicting interests' of freedom of expression and the right to private life. It stated that it wanted the emphasis to be put on encouraging the press to adhere to the provisions of the code rather than on using the PCC to 'police the code which the press are believed to be trying to get around, or as nanny to a press seen as incapable of adhering to a Code of Practice.' It also rejected certain of the proposals for reform of the PCC. It expressed the view that it was hard to see what could be gained from the introduction of a twin track complaints system and expressed scepticism about providing the PCC with power to impose financial penalties.

The Government did however concur with the Committee's conclusion that **1.62L** there was room for improvement in the system, and welcomed in particular the proposals for reform of the system of lay commissioners as likely to make the system of self regulation 'more transparent.' It also endorsed calls for improved 'branding' of published PCC adjudications.

E. The European Convention on Human Rights and The Human Rights Act 1998

The House of Lords has now confirmed that English law does not recognise any **1.63** general principle of 'invasion of privacy' from which the conditions of liability in a particular case can be deduced: *Wainwright v Home Office* [2003] 3 WLR 1137 [19]. Furthermore, the coming into force of the Human Rights Act 1998 is said to weaken the argument for saying that a general tort of invasion of privacy is needed to fill gaps in the existing remedies: [34]. The absence of a general tort of invasion of privacy should be distinguished, however, from the extension and possible renaming of the old action for breach of confidence: [30].

(2) *Absence of a Specific Law of Privacy*

Lord Hoffmann confirmed in *Wainwright v Home Office* [2003] 3 WLR 1137 **1.68** that there is nothing in the jurisprudence of the European Court of Human Rights which suggests that the adoption of some high level principle of privacy is necessary to comply with Article 8 of the Convention: [32]. His personal observation at [51], however, that Article 8 did not require a remedy for a merely negligent act which caused an invasion of privacy is hard to reconcile with the facts of *Peck v UK* (2003) 36 EHRR 41 (see further the Supplement to para 2.35 below) and other Article 8 cases such as *Craxi (No 2) v Italy*, Application 25337/94, judgment of 17 July 2003, where the precise circumstances in which private information had come into the hands of the media could not be ascertained. See further the Supplement to paras 1.76, 6.40, 12.25, and 12.31 below.

1.69 The European Court of Human Rights found violations of Articles 8 and 13 in *Peck v UK* (2003) 36 EHRR 41 where existing remedies were ineffective to compensate for an invasion of privacy caused by mass disclosure of CCTV footage of the applicant in the moments immediately following a suicide attempt in a public street. Although the BSC and ITC (but not the PCC) had upheld the applicant's complaints, their inability to award damages or grant injunctions rendered the regulators ineffective. At the relevant time (pre-HRA) the powers of a court on judicial review were too limited to give an effective remedy and the law of confidence was inapplicable on the facts. See further the supplement to para 2.35 below.

In *Wainwright v Home Office* Lord Hoffmann rejected the submission that cases like Mr Peck's demonstrated the need for a general tort of invasion of privacy. In his opinion the case showed no more than the need for a system of control of the use of film footage from CCTV cameras which shows greater sensitivity to the feelings of people who happen to have been caught by the lens. It was an area which required a detailed approach which can be achieved only by legislation rather than the broad brush of common law principle: [33]. The disadvantage with this approach, it is suggested, is that such gaps in the law are only revealed in hindsight. A good example is Parliament's attempt to fill the gap revealed by the *Malone* decision through the Interception of Communications Act 1985. This was subsequently revealed still not to comply with Article 8 because it did not apply to private telephone networks: *Halford v United Kingdom* (1997) 24 EHRR 523. Legislating in retrospect also has the potential to cause significant injustice in an individual case.

On 10 July 2003 the European Court of Human Rights declared admissible an application brought by Princess Caroline von Hannover (Application no. 59320/00) who complains that the failure of the German courts to prohibit publication of photographs of her and her children taken in public places showing scenes from her daily life (as opposed to while engaged in official duties) constitutes a breach of Article 8. The case raises in even starker form than *Spencer* the question of the extent to which public figures are entitled to respect for their private life and to control the use of their image.

1.70 See now also *Cumpana and Mazare v Romania*, Application no. 33348/96, judgment of 10 June 2003 in which the European Court held that the conviction of two journalists who were sentenced to 7 months imprisonment and banned from journalism for a year for publishing a libellous article which interfered with the victim's private life was a proportionate interference with their right to freedom of expression. See further the Supplement to paras 7.27 and 7.35 below.

(3) Margin of Appreciation

1.76 The Grand Chamber of the European Court of Human Rights gave its judgment in *Hatton v UK* on 8 July 2003. Although it reversed the finding of a violation of Article 8 it repeated the approach cited in this paragraph: (2003) 36 EHRR 51 [98]. On this occasion Sir Brian Kerr was in the majority and did not dissent from what he had previously described as 'a wholly new approach'. It would thus appear to be established, at least in the environmental field protected by Article 8, that similar considerations apply to interferences by public and private bodies.

The extent of the positive obligation under Article 8 considered in *Hatton* has now been extended into the field of disclosure of personal information by the media. In *Craxi (No 2) v Italy*, Application no. 25337/94, judgment of 17 July 2003, the European Court held that the State was under a positive obligation to prevent disclosure to the press of private information contained in court records. The documents concerned were transcripts of private telephone conversations which had been intercepted by the police for the purposes of the prosecution of the applicant, a former Prime Minister of Italy, for corruption. That duty extended to a requirement to carry out effective inquiries into the causes of the leak after it had occurred: [74]–[75]. In a partly dissenting opinion, Judge Zagrebelsky noted that this was the first occasion on which the Court had extended the positive obligation under Article 8 to include a requirement to carry out an effective investigation into its possible breach, a duty which had previously been restricted to alleged breaches of Articles 2 and 3. He pointed out that where that investigation might require, as here, disclosure of a journalist's source, it was difficult to see how it could be effective without breaching Article 10. See further the Supplement to paras 6.40, 12.25, and 12.31 below.

n210 See now also the recommendations of the Department of Culture Media **1.79** and Sport Select Committee on Media and Press Intrusion and the Government's response thereto summarised at paras 1.62A–1.62L of this Supplement above.

(4) Media Organisations as Public Authorities

n216 The decision of the Court of Appeal in *Aston Cantlow and Wilmcote with* **1.81** *Billesley Parochial Church Council v Wallbank* was reversed by the House of Lords without affecting the point made in this note: [2003] 3 WLR 283. Lord Hope stated at [37] that the Court of Appeal was right not to look to Hansard for assistance in interpreting s 6 HRA because there was no ambiguity which brought the case within the scope of the limited exception which was described in *Pepper v Hart* [1993] AC 593. Although various attempts had been made by ministers in both Houses to explain their approach to public authorities 'it is not the ministers' words, uttered as they were on behalf of the executive, that must be referred to in order to understand what Parliament intended. It is the words used by Parliament that must be examined in order to understand and apply the legislation that it has enacted.' None of their other Lordships in *Aston Cantlow* saw any proper basis for referring to Hansard as an aid to construing the term 'public authority' in s 6 either.

But Lord Roger expressed the view, however, that if assistance could properly be derived from the parliamentary debates 'it would lie in the confirmation that, in promoting the Bill, the government intended to give people rights in domestic law against the same bodies as would engage the liability of the United Kingdom before the Strasbourg court.' This was the unanimous view of the court, at least as far as 'core' public authorities are concerned (see Lord Nicholls at [6], Lord Hope at [44], Lord Hobhouse at [87], Lord Scott at [129] and Lord Roger at [160]).

In *Wilson v First County Trust Ltd* [2003] 3 WLR 568 the question arose as to whether it was permissible to have regard to Parliamentary material when exercising the court's role under the HRA of evaluating the compatibility of primary legislation with Convention rights. The Speaker of the House of Commons and Clerk of the Parliaments were given permission to intervene in the proceedings and for the first time in an English case made submissions on the use of Hansard by the courts. The House of Lords disapproved of the Court of Appeal's use of Hansard to examine Parliament's reasons for enacting s 127(3) Consumer Credit Act 1974. Having concluded that Parliament had not had sufficient justification for legislating as it had, the Court of Appeal had made a declaration of incompatibility. This was impermissible use of parliamentary material and might even be questioning parliamentary proceedings contrary to article 9 of the Bill of Rights 1689. The court was, however, entitled to have regard to parliamentary material if that was necessary in order to identify the policy objective of legislation and to assess whether the means employed to achieve that objective were proportionate to any adverse effects the legislation might have. This was part of the court's 'sociological assessment' of Parliament's response to a perceived mischief, social evil or danger which the legislation represented. This was a task which Parliament had required the courts to perform under the HRA itself: see Lord Nicholls at [61]–[67], Lord Hope at [116]–[118], and Lord Hobhouse at [140]–[145].

On the use of Hansard to construe other provisions of the Human Rights Act see further paras 10.01 n 4 and 13.136 of the Main Work and the Supplement to those paras below.

n218 In arriving at the conclusion that s 6 HRA was intended to replicate, as far as possible, the test that Strasbourg would apply in determining whether the responsibility of the State was engaged, the House of Lords in *Aston Cantlow* adopted precisely the analysis set out in this paragraph. Relying on s 7 HRA, Article 34 ECHR and the Strasbourg authorities cited in note 218 the court endorsed the view that, as far as 'core' or 'standard' public authorities are concerned, a body cannot both be under a duty to act compatibly with Convention rights under the HRA and seek to invoke them against others: see Lord Nicholls at [6]–[8], Lord Hope at [44]–[52], Lord Hobhouse at [87], and Lord Roger at [158]–[160]. This leaves 'hybrid' or 'functional' public authorities which could potentially invoke Convention rights in respect of some of their functions but be responsible for complying with them in respect of others: see *Aston Cantlow* at [9]–[11]. This may explain why both public authorities in *London Regional Transport Ltd v The Mayor of London* [2003] EMLR 88 were permitted to rely on Convention rights, the Respondent acting on this occasion in his capacity as representative of the people of London. This distinction also supports the proposition in n 226 of the Main Work that the BBC and other public service broadcasters should not be considered public authorities when exercising functions relating to journalism, art or literature, but may be for other purposes. See further the Supplement to paras 13.136 and 13.138 below.

As it did before the Court of Appeal, the BBC accepted for the purposes of its appeal to the House of Lords in *R (ProLife Alliance) v BBC* that it was a public authority, without making any wider concession as to its status in different contexts: [2003] 2 WLR 1403 at [106]. However, the House of Lords took quite a different view of its role on judicial review of the BBC's decision not to broadcast a party election broadcast by an anti-abortion party on grounds of taste and decency than had the Court of Appeal. In according to the broadcaster a much greater degree of deference than the Court below it appears that the direct application of s 6, HRA to the BBC did not add much of substance to the review. **1.82**

On the status of the BBC and other public service broadcasters in the light of the House of Lords' judgment in *Aston Cantlow and Wilmcote with Billesley Parochial Church Council v Wallbank* [2003] 3 WLR 283, see the Supplement to para 1.81 n 218 above. On the degree of deference to be paid to the decision of a public authority see the Supplement to para 13.141 n 229 below.

n226 The list of public authorities in Schedule I to the Freedom of Information Act 2000 has been added to by the Freedom of Information (Additional Public Authorities) Order 2003 (SI 2003/1882) and taken from by the Freedom of Information (Removal of References to Public Authorities) Order 2003 (SI 2003/1883) without affecting the point made in this note. The fact that the list of public authorities under the FOI Act can expand and contract shows that, as under the HRA, what constitutes a public authority is a relatively fluid concept. **1.84**

2

PRINCIPLES AND SOURCES

A. Introduction

The avoidance of disclosures or other conduct which 'would be highly offensive **2.02** to a reasonable person of ordinary sensibilities' has been accepted as a useful test, but see para 4.14 n 18 of the Main Work and the Supplement to para 6.42 n 116 below.

B. Sources

(1) Human Rights Conventions

n13 See the Supplement to paras 2.13, 7.27 and 7.35 below.   **2.06**

(2) England and Wales

(c) Personal property and confidence

The Court of Appeal has so far sought more often than not to fit the legal concept **2.12** of privacy into the existing law of breach of confidence rather than tackle the vexed question of whether there is a separate tort of invasion of privacy. This has been done whilst mindful of interpreting the law compatibly with Articles 8 and 10 of the ECHR: see *A v B plc* [2003] QB 195 at [4]: 'The court is required not to act "in a way which is incompatible with a Convention right". The court is able to achieve this by absorbing the rights which Articles 8 and 10 protect into the long-established cause of action for breach of confidence . . . giving new strength and breadth to the action'; and *Campbell v MGN Ltd* [2003] QB 658 at [43]: 'The court is in the process of identifying, on a case by case basis, the principles by which the law of confidentiality must accommodate the article 8 and 10 rights.' Beyond this, and outside the field of disclosure of personal information, the House of Lords has declined to recognise a high level tort of invasion of privacy: *Wainwright v Home Office* [2003] 3 WLR 1137.

(d) Privacy and reputation

2.13   In *Cumpana and Mazare v Romania*, Application no 33348/96, judgment of 10 June 2003, the ECtHR unanimously held that reputation and honour are equally protected by Article 8 and Article 10(2) of the Convention: see [48] and the Dissenting Opinion, last paragraph.

2.14   *X and Y v News Group Newspapers and MGN Ltd* [2003] FSR 850 and *R (Ellis) v Chief Constable of Essex Police* [2003] 2 FLR 566 illustrate the mischief which protection of privacy is designed to address. In *X and Y* an injunction was granted to give lifelong anonymity to the child killer Mary Bell and her now adult daughter. The purpose was to prevent the risk of intrusion and harassment and psychological abuse to which their notoriety would give rise (see [40]–[41], [46]–[50]). In *Ellis* the Court was invited to approve a police scheme to reduce crime by displaying poster images of selected offenders. It was not disputed that the scheme would be an interference with the offender's Article 8 rights which required to be justified as necessary under Article 8(2), the purpose of the scheme being to deter criminals from re-offending. The Court declined to rule on the legality of the particular proposal, expressing various concerns. First, the Court was concerned that the publicity might make it more difficult for the offender to obtain employment and stable accommodation on leaving prison, and thereby increase the risk of his re-offending: [33]–[34]. Second, the Court was concerned that it might result in risk of harm to the offender's children, partner, and parents, which might be an interference with their Article 8 rights: [35]. Finally the Court was concerned that the naming would justifiably be seen as a punishment, which unfairly discriminates against the offender whose name and image are selected for the scheme. The appropriate punishment will already have been imposed by the Courts, and the police have no power to impose punishment in any event: [36].

(h) Images

2.23   See now *Douglas v Hello! Ltd* [2003] 3 All ER 996, Lindsay J at [196]–[197], and para 2.14 of this Supplement. A personality right of sorts has now been recognised by the English Courts in the Court of Appeal's decision in *Irvine v Talksport* [2003] 2 All ER 881. In this false endorsement case, the Court of Appeal upheld the judgment of Laddie J that part at least of the intention was to convey a message to the audience that Talk Radio was so good that it was endorsed and listened to by Mr Eddie Irvine. Laddie J had concluded at para [75] of his judgment that:

> Mr Irvine has a property right in his goodwill which he can protect from unlicensed appropriation consisting of a false claim or suggestion of endorsement of a third party's goods or business.

In *Campbell v MGN Ltd* [2003] QB 633, [54] the Court of Appeal noted that the **2.25** reader of the newspaper in that case might have found it offensive that what were obviously covert photographs had been taken of her, but that that, of itself, was not relied upon as a ground for legal complaint. For comment on the offensiveness test see para 4.14 n18 of the Main Work and the Supplement to para 6.42 n 116 below.

(3) The European Convention on Human Rights and the Institutions of the Council of Europe

In *Campbell v MGN Ltd* at [42]–[43] the Court of Appeal stated that the Human **2.28** Rights Act has had a significant impact on the law of confidentiality. The Courts must have regard to the Article 8 right to respect for private and family life and the right to freedom of expression under Article 10. See also J Stratford, 'Striking the Balance: Privacy v. Freedom of Expression under the European Convention on Human Rights', in M. Colvin (ed), *Developing Key Privacy Rights* (2002), Ch. 2.

In *A v United Kingdom* (2003) 36 EHRR 51 the applicant complained about defamatory remarks which had been made about her and her family in Parliament in which they were described as the 'neighbours from hell'. The information disclosed by the MP included the applicant's name and address, as a result of which she received racist hate mail, and was eventually forced to move home. The European Court of Human Rights found that the absolute privilege attaching to statements made in the course of Parliamentary debates pursued such important aims so as to outweigh the applicant's right of access to court. The Court regretted the disclosure of the applicant's personal details which it said was clearly unnecessary in the context of a debate about municipal housing policy. Nevertheless, as the substance of the complaint had been dismissed under Article 6(1) the Court found no separate issue arising under Article 8.

See para 2.13 of this Supplement. In *Roemen and Schmit v Luxembourg*, **2.31** Application no 51772/99, judgment of 25 February 2003, the Court held that a search of a lawyer's offices, which produced nothing, was an interference with her right to respect for her home: [18], [72]. Furthermore, a search of a journalist's home and a newspaper's office aimed at discovering the identity of a source can constitute a violation of both Article 8 and 10: *Ernst and others v Belgium*, Application no. 33400/96, judgment of 15 July 2003. See further the Supplement to para 14.41 below.

2.35 In *Peck v United Kingdom* (2003) 36 EHRR 41 the European Court found breaches of Articles 8 and 13 of the Convention. CCTV pictures of the applicant had been used by the Local Authority without the knowledge of the applicant. The pictures showed the applicant in a distressed state after he had attempted to commit suicide by slashing his wrists. Footage was used in successive television programmes (ultimately on a BBC programme which had an audience of 9.2 million viewers). The applicant's face was unmasked or only inadequately masked. The Court held that there had been an unjustified interference with the private life of the applicant. The applicant had complained (successfully) to the Broadcasting Standards Commission and the Independent Television Commission, but unsuccessfully to the Press Complaints Commission. He failed in his complaint to the latter which took the view that since the events filmed had taken place in public, there was no infringement of any privacy right, and the coverage had been such that it did not suggest that there was any criminality in what the applicant had done, and the programme had made it clear that he was mentally unwell. An application for judicial review of this decision had failed. Since none of the remedies available to the applicant in domestic law was adequate to protect the right to private life, there was a violation of Article 13. The irrationality threshold in the case of judicial review was too high, the media commissions had no power to award damages, and the action for breach of confidence was unlikely to be available on the facts of this case. See further the Supplement to para 6.40 n 110 below.

(5) France

2.53 See C Duprée, 'The Protection of Private Life versus Freedom of Expression in French Law' in M Colvin (ed), *Developing Key Privacy Rights* (2002).

2.54 n117 The Court of Appeal in *Campbell v MGN Ltd* at [34] noted that France was one jurisdiction where it may be an actionable wrong to publish a photograph of a person taken without consent. Counsel for the claimant expressly abstained from pursuing a case that English law should recognise such a right of privacy.

(6) Germany

2.57 See R English, 'Protection of Privacy and Freedom of Speech in Germany' in M Colvin (ed), *Developing Key Privacy Rights* (2002), Ch 4.

2.58 n131 The Court of Appeal in *Campbell v MGN Ltd* at [34] noted that Germany was one jurisdiction where it may be an actionable wrong to publish a photograph of a person taken without consent. Counsel for the claimant expressly abstained from pursuing a case that English law should recognise such a right of privacy. See para 3.81 of the Main Work and *Caroline von Monaco II*, BGH NJW 1996, 1128–9. This judgment addresses photographs of celebrities taken in a variety of places, including a public park and a restaurant, and offers a persuasive application of a law of privacy with an approach similar to that adopted by the ECtHR. See further the Supplement to para 6.77 below. Following the German Constitutional Court's reversal of a similar decision in favour of Princess Caroline of 15 December 1999, the applicant has brought proceedings in Strasbourg. See further the Supplement to paras 1.69 above and 9.82–9.84 below.

(8) New Zealand

In *Hosking v Runting and others*, (HC, 30 May 2003) Randerson J declined to accede to an application for an injunction to prohibit the publication of photographs taken of the two young children of a national celebrity. The photographs were taken without the knowledge of the accompanying mother, but they were taken in a public place (a crowded shopping mall). Having surveyed the state of the law in the United Kingdom, Australia, Canada and the United States of America, and international conventions on the rights of children, the judge came to the conclusion that the New Zealand law of privacy had not developed to a point at which it conferred a free-standing cause of action in such circumstances. See further the Supplement to paras 4.12–4.14 below. See also R Tobin, 'Privacy and Freedom of Expression in New Zealand' in M Colvin (ed), *Developing Key Privacy Rights* (2002), Ch. 6.

2.63

(9) Australia

In *Campbell v MGN Ltd* the Court of Appeal adopted the *obiter dictum* of Gleeson CJ in *Australian Broadcasting Corporation v Lenah Game Meat Pty* [2001] HCA 63: see para 4.14 n18 of the Main Work and the Supplement to para 6.42 n 116 below .

2.64

In *Australian Broadcasting Corporation v Lenah Game Meats Pty* [2001] HCA 63, the High Court of Australia declined to recognise the existence of a general right of privacy. In proceedings for an injunction based on breach of confidence where the applicant's processing practices were secretly filmed by a trespasser, it was held that since access to the public was available, the activities secretly observed were not relevantly private, and the decision of the judge at first instance not to grant an injunction was upheld.

Subsequently, in *Grosse v Purvis* [2003] QDC 151 a District Court judge has held that there is an actionable civil law claim for invasion of privacy in Queensland.

Skoien J awarded substantial damages for invasion of privacy, for intentional infliction of harm under *Wilkinson v Downton* [1897] 2 QB 57, trespass and nuisance in respect of the stalking of the plaintiff by the defendant over a number of years. The judge described the recognition of a free-standing tort for invasion of privacy as a 'bold' but 'logical and desirable' step [442]. He interpreted the High Court's judgment in *Australian Broadcasting Corporation v Lenah Game Meat Pty Ltd* as identifying with sufficient clarity 'certain critical propositions . . . to found the existence of a common law cause of action for invasion of privacy' [423]. He noted that in recognising that 'the time was now right for consideration as to how and to what extent privacy should be protected at common law in Australia' [435] the High Court in *Lenah Game Meat* had relied on comparative jurisprudence including the English Court of Appeal's judgment in *Douglas v Hello! Ltd* [2001] QB 967 [434], [438]. See further the Supplement to paras 11.35–11.60 below.

See also D Lindsay, 'Freedom of Expression, Privacy and the Media in Australia' in M Colvin (ed), *Developing Key Privacy Rights* (2002), Ch. 7.

(11) Canada

2.66 See M Russell, 'The Impact of the Charter Rights on Privacy and Freedom of Expression in Canada' in M Colvin (ed), *Developing Key Privacy Rights* (2002), Ch. 5.

3

PRIVACY RIGHTS

A. Introduction

n1 However, the ECtHR is less reticent about drawing assistance from the common   **3.01**
law of other jurisdictions in order to interpret a person's Article 8 rights under the
Convention. In a recent decision it analysed judgments in Canada and Australia before deciding that the use of covert audio and video surveillance to record the conversations of a prisoner whilst he was being held in custody was a violation of his
right to privacy under Article 8, see *Allan v UK* (2003) 36 EHHR 12.

In *Campbell v MGN Ltd* [2003] QB 658 the Court of Appeal noted the distinction   **3.03**
between invasions of privacy occasioned by intrusion and those caused by disclosure
of private facts which is recognised in some other jurisdictions, such as California.
Counsel for the claimant in that case was not seeking to establish the existence in
English law of a free-standing tort of privacy based on the former category. Referring
to Prosser's analysis, Lord Hoffmann in *Wainwright v Home Office* [2003] 3 WLR
1137 [18] said that United States' jurisprudence which broke down the concept
of 'invasion of privacy' into four separate torts 'must cast doubt upon the value of
any high-level generalisation which can perform a useful function in enabling one
to deduce the rule to be applied in a concrete case'. For this and other reasons the

House of Lords confirmed that English law does not recognise a general tort of invasion of privacy capable of covering all four aspects.

B. Intrusion

(2) The United States

3.07   n12 See also *Carter v Superior Court of San Diego County; New York Times Co et al,* (Cal Ct App 4th Dist 2002), 30 Med L Rptr 1193 in which the Court, citing *Shulman,* held that the plaintiff who had been filmed whilst receiving medical treatment in hospital was 'in a zone of physical and sensory privacy and he had a reasonable expectation of privacy'.

3.09   n19 The singer and actress Barbara Streisand was recently reported as having filed a legal suit for $10million for breach of her privacy after an aerial photograph of her Malibu estate was published on a website set up by Adelman, a 39-year-old dot com millionaire who devotes his energies to protecting the environment. The photograph was shot from too far away to identify any people, but showed the back area of her house and swimming pool, which Streisand claims would leave her vulnerable to stalkers and others being able to gain information from the photograph about how to access the property. It was taken from the same distance as more than 12,000 other photos on the website that illustrate the entire California coastline and are being used to document coastal erosion and building law violations.

3.11   However, the location of the covert filming or recording seems to be a factor. So, where a cable network, in seeking to expose racism in the police force, surreptitiously filmed and recorded police officers stopping and searching an expensive-looking car driven by an undercover African-American reporter, the New Jersey Court of Appeal took the view that the officers had no reasonable expectation of privacy because the stop and search took place on the side of a public highway and was 'more akin to an open, accessible place, than an enclosed, indoor room'. There was also clearly a public interest element to this case and the Court held that officers on official police business could not expect the same level of privacy protection as a private citizen in a private place: *Hornberger v ABC Inc* 2002 WL 1058 515 (NJ Super AD) as cited in *Communications Law 2002,* (PLI, 2002), Vol 1 628.

n26 In the wake of the terrorist attacks on 11 September 2001, and the ensuing fear and paranoia of further attacks, there has been a marked increase in the number of journalists being arrested and charged for criminal trespass. In May 2002, a *Time Magazine* journalist who had disguised himself as a New York firefighter to gain access to the ground zero area of the World Trade Centre site, was charged and sentenced to 1200 hours' community service and 5 years' probation.

(4) England and Wales

(c) Harassment

In order for the criminal offence of harassment to be committed, the harassment **3.19** must be directed against an individual human being. A limited company could not be a victim under the Act: *DPP v Dziurzynski* [2002] ACD 88.

n54 The test of whether a person would think a course of conduct amounted to harassment is an objective test of what a reasonable person would think, not a hypothetical person endowed with the relevant characteristics of the defendant: see *R v Colohan* [2001] 2 FLR 757, CA where the claim for harassment was struck out as the particulars of claim disclosed no reasonable grounds for bringing the claim. On an application to strike out a claim for harassment the relevant questions are whether the claimant has established an arguable case that the conduct on the part of the defendant which is relied on is unreasonable and whether the Particulars of Claim allege more than that the defendant engaged in conduct which foreseeably caused distress to the claimant: *Sharma v Jay*, Gray J, 15 April 2003.

(d) Surreptitious Surveillance

In *Campbell v MGN Ltd* at [54] the Court of Appeal noted that the reader of the **3.21** newspaper in that case might have found it offensive that what were obviously covert photographs had been taken of her, but that that, of itself, was not relied upon as a ground for legal complaint. For comment on the offensiveness test see para 4.14 n18 of the Main Work and the Supplement to para 6.42 n 116 below. In *Douglas v Hello! Ltd* [2003] 3 All ER 996 at [205] Lindsay J held that the very same principle in the PCC Code that provides that the use of long lenses to take pictures of people in private places without their consent is unacceptable must inescapably also make the surreptitious use of short lenses to take pictures of people in private places without their consent equally unacceptable. In *Peck v United Kingdom* (2003) 36 EHRR 41, the European Court of Human Rights found that there had been a breach of Article 8, ECHR when a local authority had disclosed CCTV footage which showed Mr Peck in a public street after he had attempted to commit suicide by cutting his wrist, to various media organisations for publication without taking adequate safeguards to protect his Article 8 rights (for example by ensuring that his face was masked so that he was not identifiable). The broadcasts resulted in far greater exposure than Mr Peck could have foreseen. In *Perry v UK*, Application no 63737/00, judgment of 17 July 2003 the European Court of Human Rights found that there had been a breach of Article 8 of the Convention when police had, by a ploy, recorded footage of the applicant which they used for identification purposes, when the image had not been obtained voluntarily or in circumstances where it could be reasonably anticipated that it would be recorded and used for such purposes. There was a legal basis for the interference in the Police and Criminal Evidence Act 1984, but the failure to comply with the procedures required by the applicable Code of Practice meant that the interference was not in accordance with law. This was found to be so, and damages awarded, notwithstanding that the applicant's claim that his trial was unfair had been held inadmissible. For the current law on surreptitious surveillance and interception of communications as it affects the media see paras 11.68–11.78 of the Main Work.

C. Private Facts

(2) The United States

3.27   n76 But see *Green v CBS Broadcasting Inc*, 29 Med L Rptr 1321 (N D Tex 2000), aff'd 286 F 3d 281 (5th Cir 2002) a case in which a mother who had claimed during court proceedings that her husband had sexually abused their daughter, sued the programme *48 Hours* for publishing the allegations in the course of a programme based on the woman's divorce case. The 5th Circuit affirmed the dismissal of the private facts part of the claim on the grounds that (1) the sexual abuse allegations were stated in open court, (2) no court order was sought to protect the child's anonymity at the time of the divorce proceedings and (3) the daughter's name and likeness were a matter of public record and therefore not private.

3.30   n82 See also *Carafano v Metrosplash*, 30 Med L Rptr 1577 (C D Calif 2002), where the Court dismissed a private facts claim brought by a well-known television actress against the publishers of a matchmaking website which had posted details of her home and her address on the internet. The Court held that the information was (1) a matter of public record, (2) the actress had publicly discussed her home life in Los Angeles, thereby rendering her address 'newsworthy' and (3) there was no evidence that the defendant acted with reckless disregard as to whether or not a reasonable man would find the invasion highly offensive.

3.32   So, the singer Prince's recent private facts claim against the American *Out Magazine* for their publication of a photograph of him dancing naked from the waist up at a party, was summarily dismissed by the Second District of Appeals who found that he had no reasonable expectation of privacy whilst at a party, even where the party organisers had assured his privacy, because the party was open to members of the public who purchased a ticket, the party was attended by at least 1,000 people, and he was dancing in full view of all those attending the party: *Prince v Out Publishing*, 2002 Cal App LEXIS 25 (3 January 2002) as cited in *Communications Law 2002*, 688.

Thus, in a claim arising out of the publication in the book *A Civil Action* that **3.35** the claimant was suffering from depression during toxic waste litigation, the Court upheld the dismissal of the private facts claim on the grounds that the fact was substantially relevant to the litigation and the litigation was a matter of legitimate public interest. The Court took the view that even if a fact taken on its own may not be newsworthy, its publication would be protected by the First Amendment if it was related to a newsworthy topic: *Riley v Harr*, 292 F 2d 382 (1st Cir 2002), cited in *Communications Law 2002*, 818.

D. False Light

(1) Introduction

n110 See *Schiavarelli v CBS*, No 992009185 (Ill Cir Ct Cook County, October **3.42** 2001) and *Muzikowski v Paramount Pictures Corporation, et al*, 2001 US, Dist LEXIS 19397 (N Dist Ill Nov 28, 2001). Illinois has recently joined those states that have precluded corporations from asserting false light claims.

(2) The United States

(b) Distortion

In the case of *Solano, Jr v Playgirl Inc* No.CV 00-01242 DT (Ex) (C D Cal, Feb **3.50** 27, 2001), rev'd 2002 WL 1291240 (9th Cir 2002), as cited in *Communications Law 2002*, 643, the 9th Circuit reinstated a false light claim brought by an actor, known for his role on the television series *Baywatch*. The magazine published a photograph of him semi-naked on their cover with the headlines 'Primetime's Sexy Young Star Exposed' and 'Baywatch's Best Body, Jose Solano'. Other headlines included ones stating that the magazine contained plenty of photographs of graphic male frontal nudity. The plaintiff argued that taken as a whole, this cover conveyed the false impression that he had posed and consented to publication of nude photographs of himself in a pornographic magazine. There was sufficient evidence of malice (there was evidence that some members of the editorial team had deliberately and knowingly created a false impression in order to boost sale figures) to allow the claim to proceed.

E. Personality and Publicity Rights

(2) The United States

n180 The full citation for the *Comedy III Productions* case should conclude 'cert **3.75** denied 122 S Ct 806 (US Cal 2002)'.

3.76   It has also been held that use of a person's image in artwork displayed in a public art gallery was 'speech' in the form of artistic expression, and not being used for the purposes of advertising and trade, was protected by the First Amendment. In *Hoepker v Kruger*, 2001 WL 987937, 336 (SDNY 2001) a claim for copyright infringement and misappropriation under New York Civil Rights Law ss 50–51 failed. It was brought against the artist and museum that exhibited art work containing an altered photograph of the plaintiff in a collage piece. This decision expanded the 'newsworthiness' protection which attaches to some types of a person's name and likeness when used in books and magazines, to works of art as well as material used to disseminate that work (ie posters, postcards, and other souvenirs). See also *Tyne et al v Time Warner Entertainment Co* 204, F Supp 2d 1338 (MD Fla 2002), a claim at common law and under Florida Statute for misappropriation of names, images and likenesses of the families and survivors of the drowned crew members of the fishing vessel, 'Andrea Gail', the subject of the film *The Perfect Storm*. The Court granted the defendants summary judgment stating that the statutory claim failed because the use was expressive and not commercial. The Court also held that the film constituted 'speech' and the appropriation of the names, images and likenesses of the plaintiffs were used to depict events which were of legitimate public interest.

(3) Canada

3.77   *Aubry v Les Editions Vice-Versa Inc* [1998] 1 SCR 591 is discussed in the New Zealand case of *Hosking v Runting*, HC, 30 May 2003. The High Court of New Zealand pointed out that the Court in *Aubry* had balanced the right to privacy under the Quebec Charter against the right in s 3 of the Charter to freedom of expression and discussed this analysis at [111]–[112]. Further, the High Court concluded at [113] that 'although the *Aubry* case is helpful in identifying the values underpinning the right to privacy guaranteed by the Quebec charter, it does not support a general cause of action based on a free-standing privacy tort. No such tort has been recognised in Canada.'

The right identified in *Aubry* has been developed in subsequent cases decided by the Supreme Court of Quebec. The applicable principles in establishing such a right were recently restated in *Brisson v Virtually Magazine*, SC, 27 June 2002. The case concerned a family who had been photographed at a naturist camp, with the photographs subsequently appearing in a magazine. Although the photographs had been taken consensually, the family had expected to have final approval of the pictures before publication, and were awarded 6,000 Canadian Dollars. The Supreme Court stated that to succeed in such a claim, a claimant must prove that his image was actually published and was recognisable in the photograph(s) published. Both causation and damage must be proved as there is no presumption of damage when an image right as defined in *Aubry* has been breached.

(6) England and Wales

(a) Copyright

n207 See eg *A v B and C*, QBD, 2 March 2001 referred to in the Supplement to **3.86**
para 3.104 below.

(b) Passing off

A person's voice can also attract protection under the law of passing off: see, eg *Sim* **3.89**
v Heinz [1959] 1 All ER 547, CA.

Irvine v Talksport Ltd [2003] 2 All ER 881 was heard by the Court of Appeal on **3.91**
both liability and quantum. The defendant's appeal on liability was dismissed, but
the claimant's appeal as to quantum was allowed, and the Court substituted the
award of £2,000 with an award of £25,000. The Court held that the judge had
misunderstood the evidence on what a reasonable licence fee would have been—
that being the relevant test for damages in a case for false endorsement (see *General
Tire and Rubber Company v Firestone Tyre and Rubber Company* [1976] RPC 197).

(d) Breach of confidence

Considerable doubt was cast on *Times Newspapers v MGN Ltd* by Lindsay J in **3.95**
Douglas v Hello! Ltd, [2003] 3 All ER 996 [224]: 'I do not regard *Times Newspapers*
as authoritative in the post Human Rights Act age.' The Court dismissed the
proposition in *Times Newspapers* that an intention to publish destroyed the confidential nature of information. *Ashdown v Telegraph Group Ltd* [2002] Ch 149, CA
is an important decision in copyright in relation to unpublished works. The
Court clarified the extent to which a fair dealing defence within the current events
exception under s 30, CPDA 1988 could be relied upon in relation to an unpublished work. Relying on human rights case law, and the principle of proportionality, the Court held that use of an unpublished work was permitted under the fair
dealing defence, but limited to that necessary to establish authenticity.

At trial, Lindsay J upheld the claimants' claims for breach of confidence in *Douglas* **3.96**
v Hello! Ltd. The Court considered the couple's wedding pictures as 'a valuable
trade asset, a commodity the value of which depended, in part at least, upon its
content at first being kept secret and then of its being made public in ways con-
trolled by Miss Zeta-Jones and Mr Douglas for the benefit of them and of the 3rd
Claimant' [196].

The Judge recognised that:

> such an approach may lead to the distinction between the circumstances in which
> equity affords protection to those who seek to manage their publicity as part of their
> trade or profession and whose private life is a valuable commodity and those whose

is not but I am untroubled by that; the law which protects individual confidences and a law of privacy may protect the latter class and provide no reason to diminish protection for the former.

In fact, *OK!* magazine's rights to the exclusivity of photographic coverage of the wedding was considered 'even more plainly a right in the nature of a trade secret'.

The Court found that the security measures taken by the Douglases, and the clear prohibition on photography at their wedding meant that the photographer who took the pictures featured in *Hello!* magazine came under a duty of confidence. The circumstances in which *Hello!* acquired the photographs tainted its conscience, as the publishers were well aware that there would be strict security measures at the wedding, and that *OK!* had secured an exclusive deal which would contain provisions to preserve the secrecy of the event.

All of *Hello!*'s defences were rejected. In particular, the complaint that what the claimants were seeking to do was not to preserve rights of confidentiality and privacy, but to *control* their publicity. The Court considered that this was no defence—the essence of trade secrets cases is that the claimant does indeed want to control exploitation and to make information public as and when he chooses and in the circumstances selected by him.

3.101   On the issue of the offence caused by taking covert photographs see the Supplement to paras 3.21 above and 6.52 below.

3.104   The case of *A v B and C*, QBD, 2 March 2001 is also of interest. The case concerned a pop star who posed for pornographic shots a few years before her rise to fame. She had hoped the photographs would be distributed within the industry, with the aim of generating work for her, but she told the photographer that they were only to be used with her consent. Once she achieved fame, publishers obtained copyright in the pictures and licensed them to a newspaper. The pop star successfully obtained an injunction preventing a newspaper from printing the photographs, on the basis of the contractual arrangement between the pop star and the photographer, and on grounds of breach of confidence.

(e) Anonymity

3.105   n243 But where a set of circumstances arise which are not covered by statute, though the court should be slow to extend the incursion into the right of free speech by the use of inherent jurisdiction, it does have a general 'protective jurisdiction'. This could be applied in circumstances where the information relates to events within a child's recent family life in which he was directly involved and which would continue to have a serious impact upon the way in which he would be brought up. Thus, in *Re S (publicity)* [2003] HRLR 911, although the information sought to be restrained related to the identity of the defendant and victim in a murder trial, this added dimension did not take it out of the category where no jurisdiction existed. In this case, though the Court of Appeal held that it could exercise its jurisdiction to restrain the publication of the identity of a defendant and her victim in a murder trial to protect the privacy of S who was the subject of care proceedings, it decided it would not do so on this occasion. The Court considered that this was not a case where the child's welfare was the paramount consideration as care proceedings had already taken place. In carrying out a balancing exercise between Articles 8 and 10 (and taking into account Article 6) it could be seen that as knowledge of the incident and the identity of the parties were already in the public domain, anonymity would only have a mitigating effect. On the other hand there was a clear and proper interest in knowing the name of the defendant in a murder trial.

It has now been accepted that in certain exceptional circumstances worldwide injunctions restraining the identification of certain individuals can be granted where, if the injunction was not granted, there would be a risk of the applicant's Article 8 rights being breached. In *X and Y v News Group Newspapers and MGN Ltd* [2003] FSR 850, Butler-Sloss P granted an injunction *contra mundum* preventing the reporting of identification or whereabouts of Mary Bell, a convicted murderer, and her daughter. It was accepted that unlike in *Venables v News Group Newspapers Ltd* [2001] Fam 430, the applicants' rights under Articles 2 and 3 of the Convention were not likely to be breached as a result of their identification. However, the Court held that there were exceptional reasons which justified making the order on the basis of a risk of breach of Article 8, in particular, the state of X's mental health and the fact that her mental illness would be seriously exacerbated if she were to be identified. The position of the mother and daughter were found to be so intertwined that it was impossible to look at either of them in isolation. To grant an injunction to one and to refuse it to the other would have been unworkable in reality. In making the order, the Court took into account the fact that there was only a limited amount of information which required protection and that there was sufficient information in the public domain for the press and other parts of the media to be able to comment freely on the relevant aspects of the case. **3.106–3.107**

The more limited power to sell the electoral register for use by credit reference agencies was held not to be an infringement of Article 8, because the use of the electoral roll for these purposes is in the public interest: *R (Robertson) v Secretary of State for the Home Department* [2003] EWHC 1760 (Admin). **3.109**

4

PUBLICATION OF PERSONAL INFORMATION

A. Introduction

(1) Development and Sources of a 'Privacy' Law

It is increasingly apparent that the courts will develop and apply the common law **4.05** in preference to the Data Protection Act 1998 in cases where either the common law or the statute might be applied. Referring to *Venables and Thompson v News Group Newspapers Ltd and others* [2001] Fam 430 and *X and others v News Group Newspapers Ltd* [2003] FSR 850 (where the President made orders protecting the identity and whereabouts of Thompson and Venables, and of Mary Bell and her daughter), Lord Phillips MR said in *Re S (Publicity)* [2003] HRLR 911 [99]: 'These two decisions . . . exemplify . . . the manner in which the courts have extended both the scope of confidential information and the use of the injunction to protect this, thereby giving effect to the right to respect for private life conferred by Article 8 of the Human Rights Convention.' Cases where the Data Protection Act 1998 was held to add nothing of significance include *R (Ellis) v Chief*

Constable of Essex Police [2003] 2 FLR 566 [29] and *Douglas v Hello! Ltd* [2003] 3 All ER 996, at [239]. In *Re S (Publicity)* [2003] HRLR 911 [49] Hale LJ considered that where a publication increased an already substantial risk of a child developing mental illness later in life, then his rights both to family and to private life were engaged.

n 7 The incremental approach to protection of privacy was also favoured by the House of Lords in *Wainwright v Home Office* [2003] 3 WLR 1137. Their Lordships recognised that there are gaps in the protection of privacy afforded by English law; 'cases in which the courts have considered that an invasion of privacy deserves a remedy which the existing law does not offer' [18]. Those gaps can be filled in some areas by 'judicious development of an existing principle' [18]. One example is the developing law of breach of confidence. Other gaps can only be filled by legislation. The limits of judicial development are obscure but it appears that legislation is needed in areas which require 'a detailed approach' [33] such as telephone tapping [21] and the regulation of CCTV film [33].

(a) Arguments in favour of further development of the common law

4.08   See the Supplement to para 13.02 below.

(b) Arguments against further development of the common law

4.12–4.14   In *Hosking v Runting* (HC, 30 May 2003) the High Court in New Zealand declined to recognise a free-standing common law privacy tort. Randerson J gave five reasons for his decision at [118]:

(a)   The deliberate approach taken by the legislature to date on privacy issues suggests that the courts should be cautious about creating new law in this field;

(b)   The tort contended for by the plaintiffs goes well beyond the limited form of the tort recognised in decisions of this court to date and is not supported by principle or authority;

(c)   Existing remedies are likely to be sufficient to meet most claims to privacy based on the public disclosure of private information and to protect children whose privacy may be infringed without such disclosure;

(d)   In the light of subsequent developments, it is difficult to support the privacy cases decided in New Zealand to date;

(e)   To the extent there may be gaps in privacy law, they should be filled by the legislature, not the courts.

The case involved the publication of photographs of the claimants' children taken in a public place. The claimants were media stars in New Zealand and had recently separated. The claimants sued the photographer and a magazine publisher contending that the taking of the photographs and/or their publication without consent was a breach of their children's right of privacy. The case raised the controversial question of whether photographs that were arguably private in nature could be protected by the law of confidence because they were taken in a public place. The Court distinguished *Peck v UK* (2003) 36 EHRR 41 on the grounds that the case 'depended on the application of specific privacy provisions of the European Convention and involved the publication of material likely to be highly offensive to reasonable persons of ordinary sensibility given the very personal and distressing circumstances in which Mr Peck found himself': [135].

Save for the extension and possible renaming of the old action for breach of confidence, the House of Lords adopted a similar approach in *Wainwright v Home Office* [2003] 3 WLR 1137 and declined to recognise a high level tort of invasion of privacy in English law. The renaming of the cause of action for invasions of privacy caused by disclosure of personal information must wait for another day: [30].

The Culture, Media & Sport Select Committee called for Parliament to legislate for a privacy law (5th Report of Session 2002–2003 HC 458-1, *Privacy & Media Intrusion*, para 34):

> On balance we firmly recommend that the Government reconsider its position and bring forward legislative proposals to clarify the protection that individuals can expect from unwarranted intrusion by anyone—not the press alone—into their private lives. This is necessary fully to satisfy the obligations upon the UK under the European Convention of Human Rights. There should be full and wide consultation but in the end Parliament should be allowed to undertake its proper legislative role.

The Secretary of State responded confirming that the Government has no plans to legislate in this area. See further paras 1.62I–1.62L in this Supplement.

B. Types of Information

(5) Types of Personal Information Protected by Codes Regulating the Media

The Communications Act 2003 received Royal Assent on 17 July 2003. On 29 December 2003, the regulatory functions of the Broadcasting Standards Commission, the Radio Authority and Independent Television Commission transfer to Ofcom. From that point, the BBC falls under the jurisdiction of an external regulator with the power to fine it for contraventions of the Code. Ofcom will adopt a new regulatory Code which will set standards on the content of programmes to be included in television and radio services as appear to them best calculated to secure the various standards objectives set out in s 319 Communications Act. But the provisions of the Code on fairness and privacy made under s 107 Broadcasting Act 1996 will remain unchanged until Ofcom

4.31

chooses to revise them: s 2 and Schedule 1, Clause 14. See further the Supplement to para 13.01 below.

C. Dissemination of Private Information

4.34–4.43   Two decisions of the Court of Appeal have analysed the meaning of 'publication' in the context of the Administration of Justice Act, s 12. In *Re M (A Child) (Children and Family Reporter: Disclosure)* [2003] Fam 26 [21], [65]–[67] the Court held that 'publication' in the Act differed from the meaning of publication for the purposes of defamation, in that a communication between two professionals exchanging information in the course of their respective functions, each acting in furtherance of the protection of children, does not constitute a publication breaching the privacy of contemporaneous Children Act proceedings. 'Publication' was to be given the ordinary meaning of giving publicity. However, in *Re G (A Child) (Disclosure: Prohibition)* [2003] EWCA Civ 1055 the Court of Appeal held that although in *Re M* the Court had decided that an oral communication to a child protection officer did not amount to publication, 'it does not follow that an oral statement by one individual to another cannot amount to publication. All depends on the surrounding facts and circumstances.' Thorpe LJ (who was also a judge in *Re M*) continued at [26]:

> At paragraph 21 of my judgment in *Re M* I referred without citation to paragraph 8-79 of the second edition of Arlidge, Eady and Smith on Contempt. The meaning of publication in section 12 is thus explained by the authors:
>
> > Unless it is clear from the statutory context that some other interpretation is intended, it is submitted that the wide interpretation of the common law, and particularly the law of defamation, would be the natural one to adopt. That is to say, the 'publication' contemplated by section 12(1) would not be confined to information communicated through the media. Thus private communications to individuals may very well constitute contempt unless permission has previously been obtained from the Court itself
>
> That seems to me to be the sensible construction and I would adopt it.

No specific attention was paid to the issue of publication in *Lady Archer v Williams* [2003] FSR 869. The defendant, Lady Archer's former personal assistant, had been attempting to sell her story about working with Lady Archer. Before an interlocutory injunction had been granted, the defendant had only sent a fax to a journalist working for the *News of The World* outlining the nature of the story she was prepared to sell. Prior to doing so, the journalist had provided an undertaking that he would not publish anything he learned until such time as agreement was reached about payment for the story. However, before any such agreement could be reached, *The Sunday Mirror* published material which the judge found must have come from the fax, possibly as a result of its being copied to Max Clifford, who was negotiating on the defendant's behalf with various newspapers.

The defendant contended that she was not responsible for the publication in *The Sunday Mirror*. Jackson J accepted the defendant's evidence that she had not had any contact with *The Sunday Mirror* and that she had not authorised Max Clifford to release any information to *The Sunday Mirror*. Nevertheless, he held that she was responsible for the publication, stating at [72]:

> The defendant had embarked upon a high risk strategy. In breach of her duty to the claimant, the defendant disclosed confidential information in substantial quantities to Max Clifford, a public relations consultant; Mr. Henderson of the Mail on Sunday; Mr. Kellaway of News of the World; and journalist Y of the Daily Mail. The defendant had been told both by Mr. Henderson and by Mr. Kellaway that the topics covered in her 13 page fax were of particular interest to the press. Mr. Clifford was using his contacts in the media world to find a buyer for this information. It must have been obvious to anyone in the defendant's position that there was a substantial risk that, one way or another, the information which she was disclosing would find its way into the newspapers.

It is not apparent from the reports available at the time of preparation of this Supplement whether, in making the finding of responsibility for publication, the Court considered the defamation authorities on the point. In *McManus v Beckham* [2002] 1 WLR 2982 the Court of Appeal set out the conditions on liability for further publication. Waller LJ at [34] put the test as follows:

> If a defendant is actually aware (1) that what she says or does is likely to be reported, and (2) that if she slanders someone that slander is likely to be repeated in whole or in part, there is no injustice in her being held responsible for the damage that the slander causes via that publication. I would suggest further that if a jury were to conclude that a reasonable person in the position of the defendant should have appreciated that there was a significant risk that what she said would be repeated in whole or in part in the press and that that would increase the damage caused by the slander, it is not unjust that the defendant should be liable for it. Thus I would suggest a direction along the above lines rather than by reference to 'foreseeability'.

Laws LJ at [43] put it thus:

> It will not however in my judgment be enough to show that D's slander is a cause of X's further publication: for such a cause might exist although D could have no reason to know of it; and then to hold D responsible would not be just. This is why the old formula, 'natural and probable cause', is inapt even as a figurative description of the relationship that needs to be shown between D's slander and the further publication if D is to be held liable for the latter. It must rather be demonstrated that D foresaw that the further publication would probably take place, or that D (or a reasonable person in D's position) should have so foreseen and that in consequence increased damage to C would ensue.

Clarke LJ agreed with both judgments at [36].

Given the admitted publication to the *News of the World* journalist, the point had no relevance to the defendant's liability or the claim for an injunction, but it was relevant to damages (albeit that the Court's award of damages was very modest in any event). See the Supplement to para 10.107 below.

D. Liability for Publication

(1) Generally

4.44 A separate question from the meaning of publication (ie what constitutes disclosure or publication?), is responsibility for publication (ie who counts as a wrong-doer, when publication has in fact occurred?). In *Douglas v Hello! Ltd* [2003] EMLR 585 [33] (on appeal from Laddie J) the CA held that there was a good arguable case that the author of a photograph is as much a joint tortfeasor responsible for its publication in breach of a duty of confidentiality or a right of privacy as an author of a written piece would be jointly liable with its publishers in a suit for libel. See to the same effect *Douglas v Hello! Ltd* [2003] EMLR 601 Morritt V-C [72] in relation to others alleged to be involved in the publication of the photographs.

(2) Jurisdiction

4.47 n96 Dow Jones & Co Inc's appeal from the Victorian Supreme Court decision was refused by the High Court of Australia which rejected the single publication rule: [2002] HCA 56.

(3) Conflict of Law

4.49 Questions of applicable law commonly arise in relation to international publications. Whether privacy is a tort or not will be of practical importance in considering the applicable law under the Private International Law (Miscellaneous Provisions) Act 1995, s 11. In an interlocutory appeal on a challenge to jurisdiction by the supplier of the photographs in *Douglas v Hello! Ltd* [2003] EMLR 585 [41] (on appeal from Laddie J), the CA held there was a good arguable case that the proper law of the tort (or of the right in restitution for breach of the duty of confidentiality) was in effect the law of the place of publication for the purposes of s 11(1) and (2)(c), citing *Dicey & Morris on The Conflict of Laws* (13th edn, 2000), at 34R-001 (Rule 200(2)(c)) and 34-032/6.

The editors of *Clerk & Lindsell on Torts* (18th edn, 2000) support characterising such claims as torts: paras 1.01, 1.02, 1.12 and 1.34. If the claim is equitable, *Dicey & Morris* suggest that the applicable law is the law of the country where enrichment occurs: *The Conflict of Laws* (13th edn) para 34-009 (9). The general rule in relation to torts involving communication of information is that the tort is

complete where the communication is received and understood: *Dow Jones &
Company Inc v Gutnick* [2002] HCA 56 (10 December 2002), *Berezovsky v Forbes
Inc* [2000] 1 WLR 1004, *Cordoba Shipping v National Bank (The Albaforth)*
[1984] 2 Lloyd's Rep 91. In *Douglas v Hello! Ltd* [2003] EMLR 585 [33] (on appeal from Laddie J) the CA held that it did not matter that there may well have
been an earlier breach of the duty of confidentiality or invasion of the right of privacy at the time when the photographs were first taken in the Plaza Hotel in New
York, nor that such earlier wrongs may have been governed by the law of the state
of New York.

In *Douglas v Hello! Ltd* [2003] 3 All ER 996, at [277] Lindsay J noted the absence
of any evidence that any of those involved in the UK publication while themselves
being abroad credibly asserted a belief that what had been done should not be
complained of because it was not offensive under local law. He further stated that
he did not see that publication in the UK would have been any less uncon-
scionable had the publication in New York been lawful.

(4) Parties

(b) **Children**

In *Re S (Publicity)* [2003] HRLR 911 the Court of Appeal considered the juris- **4.52**
diction of the High Court in cases involving the care and upbringing of children
over whose welfare the Court is exercising a supervisory role. In that case the issue
was: can or should the Court restrain the publication of the identity of a defendant
and her victim in a murder trial to protect the privacy of her son who is the subject of care proceedings? This was not a case in which the child's welfare was the
paramount consideration: [22]. The Court unanimously adopted the view that
the jurisdiction to restrain the publication existed ([40], [100]) and (as expressed
by Latham LJ at [75]–[76]) that:

> the jurisdiction is, as Ward LJ said in *re* Z and Millett LJ said in *R v Central
> Television plc*, theoretically unlimited, but that as Waite LJ said in the latter case at
> page 207, 'The courts have nevertheless found it necessary to set self-imposed lim-
> its upon its exercise.' It seems, to me, however, that the limitations so far imposed
> on its exercise have to be reconsidered in the light of the Human Rights Act 1998.
> As there is a proper foundation for the court to exercise jurisdiction, the child's
> rights under Article 8 must be taken into account by the court if it is to comply
> with its obligations under Section 6 of the Act. It follows that the court is at least
> entitled to consider the grant of an injunction in cases such as this even if public-
> ity is not directed at the child or his carers and could not be shown to have an ad-
> verse effect on the care proceedings, although that will undoubtedly be a
> significant factor in deciding whether or not an injunction should ultimately be
> granted. This conclusion has the added benefit of enabling the family court to
> make an order in an appropriate case if it is clear that the criminal court would have
> made an order under section 39 of the Children and Young Persons Act 1933 but

for the fact that, for what may be wholly fortuitous reasons, the child in question is not a witness or does not happen to be a victim identified in the indictment. It follows that in considering whether or not to make an order such as the order applied for in the present case, the Court has to carry out the exercise which was identified at . . . [[55]–[57] and [65] ie of identifying the extent to which refusing to grant the relevant terms of the injunction asked for would be a proportionate interference with the private life of the child on the one hand and their grant would be a proportionate interference with the rights of the press under Article 10 on the other hand]. In doing so, the court will have to bear in mind on the one hand the effect that publicity will have on the child, and the extent to which it will affect the ability of the court to carry out its obligations to the child in the exercise of its care jurisdiction on the one hand, and the effect that the order will have on the ability of the press to provide the public with a full and fair report of the proceedings bearing in mind the interest which the public has in knowing the identity of a defendant, which is one of the important and usually inevitable consequences of a public trial. In addition, in a case such as the present, the court will need to take into consideration the extent of the protection which Parliament has provided in section 39 of the Children and Young Persons Act 1933, which gives the press a discretion as to how to report a case in order to give effect to that protection. And it should bear in mind the cautionary words of Glidewell LJ in *ex parte Crook* [1995] 1 WLR 139 at page 145 A to B [ie: as a general proposition there is a strong and proper public interest in knowing the identity of those who have committed crimes, particularly serious and detestable crimes, and that orders preventing the disclosure of the identity of defendants or other persons concerned in criminal proceedings should only be made when they are justified].

In the event the injunction was refused on the grounds that it was already well known in the area in which he lived that the child's mother had been charged and was to be tried for the murder of the child's brother. Anonymity would therefore only have, if anything, a mitigating effect. On the other hand, there was a clear and proper public interest in knowing the name of the defendant in such a trial.

At [61] Hale LJ said: 'The Crown Court, as a creature of statute, does not have that jurisdiction, nor does any judge have it simply by virtue of sitting in the Crown Court. But a judge who is authorised, either by virtue of his office as a High Court judge, or under section 9 of the Supreme Court Act 1981, to sit in the Family Division of the High Court could do so in that capacity.'

In *Hosking v Runting* (New Zealand High Court, Randerson J, 30 May 2003), the Court suggested at [150] that a child might have a more restricted expectation of privacy if his/her parents had courted publicity. However, this would appear to confuse the rights of the child with the actions of the parents (over which the child will usually have no control at all).

(c) Dead persons

4.55 Some rights of privacy survive permanent loss of consciousness. In *Airedale NHS*

Trust v Bland [1993] AC 789, 829, Hoffmann LJ said: 'It is demeaning to the human spirit to say that, being unconscious, he can have no interest in his personal privacy and dignity, in how he lives or dies.'

In *Craxi (No 2) v Italy*, Application no 25337/94, judgment of 17 July 2003, the European Court of Human Rights held that the deceased applicant's widow, son and daughter had standing to continue the proceedings under Article 8 in the applicant's stead, and held that the award of two thousand Euros for non-pecuniary loss be paid to the applicant's heirs: para 90 of the judgment and para 4 of the Order.

The Press Complaints Commission has considered a complaint by the Tolkien family (26 January 2003, Report 62) that articles published in a regional newspaper alleging that John Tolkien (deceased) was a paedophile were inaccurate in breach of Clause 1 (Accuracy) and intrusive in breach of Clauses 3 (Privacy) and 5 (Intrusion into grief or shock) of the Code. The PCC upheld the complaints under Clause 5 but rejected the complaints under Clause 3. The PCC decided that it was not possible to invade the privacy of someone who was dead and that the articles themselves did not invade the privacy of the surviving relatives. It stated:

> ... the Commission did not consider that questions of privacy and intrusion could relate to the deceased or that, as publication had been subsequent to the death of Father Tolkien, it could consider this aspect of the complaint further. Additionally, it made clear its view that the articles themselves had not intruded specifically into the private lives of other members of the Tolkien family in breach of the Code.

See also *R v Broadcasting Complaints Commission, ex p Granada Television Ltd* [1995] EMLR 163, the facts of which are set out at para 13.45 of the Main Work.

E. Intentional Infliction of Harm

n128 see also *P v D* [2000] 2 NZLR 591 and *Hosking v Runting* (New Zealand **4.72** High Court, Randerson J, 30 May 2003)

The House of Lords in *Wainwright v Home Office* [2003] 3 WLR 1137 effectively **4.83–4.88** declared that the action in *Wilkinson v Downton* is now redundant in the light of developments in the law of negligence and the enactment of the Protection from Harassment Act 1997. Where an actual psychiatric injury (such as Post Traumatic Stress Disorder) is caused by the careless act of another then damages will be recoverable for nervous shock caused by negligence. But where the damage falls short of a recognised medical injury (as is the case with distress or anxiety) the situation is different. Parliament has provided in the Protection from Harassment Act 1997 a statutory cause of action for the intentional infliction of such emotional harm where it results from a course of conduct (meaning conduct on at least two occasions). Lord Hoffmann did not resile from his proposition in *Hunter v Canary Wharf* that the policy considerations which limit the heads of recoverable damage in negligence do not apply equally to torts of intention, but wished to reserve his opinion as to whether a single act of harassment should sound in damages at common law: 'The requirement of a course of conduct shows that Parliament was conscious that it might not be in the public interest to allow the law to be set in motion for one boorish incident. It may be that any development of the common law should show similar caution' [46].

If a single act were to give rise to damages, Lord Hoffmann said it is necessary to be clear what is meant by intend: 'In *Wilkinson v Downton* RS Wright J wanted to water down the concept of intention as much as possible. He clearly thought, as the Court of Appeal did afterwards in *Janvier v Sweeney* [1919] 2 KB 316, that the plaintiff should succeed whether the conduct of the defendant was intentional or negligent. But the *Victorian Railway Comrs* case 13 App Cas 222 prevented him from saying so. So he devised a concept of imputed intention which sailed as close to negligence as he felt he could go' [44]. The concept of 'imputed intent' will not suffice if the law is going to draw a principled distinction which justifies abandoning the rule that damages for mere distress are not recoverable. 'The defendant must actually have acted in a way which he *knew to be unjustifiable* and intended to cause harm or at least acted without caring whether he caused harm or not' [45] (emphasis added).

Thus, there may still be limited scope for development of a common law cause of action for an intentional act which causes emotional harm, providing the defendant was acting in a way which he knew to be unjustifiable. This requirement is vague and likely to be difficult to prove. It is clearly a subjective test and circumstances from which such a state of mind could be inferred may be few and far between. In *Wainwright* itself Lord Scott stated [57]: 'whether or not it was the intention of the prison officers to humiliate and cause distress to Mrs Wainwright and to Alan, it must, in my opinion, be accepted that the manner in which the strip searches were carried out was calculated (in an objective sense) to produce and did in fact, in relation to each of them, produce that result.' Thus, not being aware of the obvious consequences of your actions is insufficient. This may be in line with recent developments in the definition of recklessness in respect of serious criminal offences (a person does not act recklessly unless he is aware of a risk that a result will occur and it is, in all the circumstances, unreasonable to take the risk: *R v G and another* [2003] 3 WLR 1060, where the offence was arson under s 1 Criminal Damage Act 1971) but it is questionable whether such an approach is necessary or appropriate in the civil law. In fact, in over-ruling *R v Caldwell* and moving to a subjective test of recklessness in *R v G* the House of Lords expressly stated that they were not addressing the meaning of 'reckless' in any other statutory or common law context (see Lord Bingham at [28]).

In *Re S (Publicity)* [2003] HRLR 911 it was argued that Article 8 adds nothing in **4.89** a case against newspapers, because they are not public authorities, and that the Court can only strike a balance between the countervailing rights of individuals under Article 8 and of the media under Article 10 in an action for breach of confidence: see *Douglas v Hello! Ltd* [2001] QB 967, and *A v B plc* [2003] QB 195 [4]. This argument was rejected: [48]. Hale LJ said an action for breach of confidence cannot be the only context in which the courts have to strike a fair balance between the rights of individuals under Article 8 and Article 10. While the courts cannot invent a new cause of action between private persons, the same issues arise whenever it has jurisdiction to restrain publication. It would appear to follow that the same issues would arise when the interference with the private or family rights of the individual were by means other than publication.

5

DATA PROTECTION AND THE MEDIA

A. Introduction

n 3 See the Supplement to para 3.109 above.   **5.01**

B. Data Protection

(1) Property in Personal Information

n7 The European Court of Human Rights found that the failure of the English   **5.04**
judicial review proceedings to afford Mr Peck a remedy for the invasion of privacy
caused by the publication of the CCTV footage amounted to a breach of Article
13. See the Supplement to para 1.69 above.

(2) Freedom of Expression—Tension or Conflict?

In *Campbell v MGN Ltd* [2003] QB 633, [97], [110]–[112] the Court of Appeal   **5.05**
accepted that the right to freedom of expression referred to in Recital 37 and Article
9 of the Directive must inform the interpretation of the Data Protection Act 1998.
The Court held at [128] that the media exemption in s 32 applies not only to the
period before publication, but is of general application: see the Supplement to
para 5.80 below. It remains open to question whether that interpretation of s 32 is

41

sufficient to give effect to Article 10, ECHR in relation to data protection, or whether some more general Article 10 defence will have to be recognised. The Court of Appeal stated at [124] that, in the absence of s 32, the requirements of the Act would impose restrictions on the media which would radically restrict freedom of the press. As discussed at para 5.79 of the Main Work, s 32 is an exemption which applies to personal data which are processed only for journalism, literature, and the arts. The exemption afforded by that section would therefore not apply to disclosures in other circumstances, even those where freedom of expression is of particular importance, for example at an election, or at a public meeting, or in a document distributed for the purpose of political debate. The reasoning of the Court of Appeal would seem to imply the need for a defence based on freedom of expression in some cases not covered by s 32. For a discussion of the effect of Article 10 on DPA 1998 see the works referred to at para 5.04 n5 of the Main Work.

In *Durant v Financial Services Authority* [2003] EWCA Civ 1746 [3], [47] the Court of Appeal accepted that the Directive 'is an important aid to construction of the Act' and that the DPA 1998 'should . . . be interpreted, so far as possible in the light of, and to give effect to, the Directive's provisions.' The Court held that the Directive's primary objective was to protect an individual's right to privacy, as enshrined in Article 8 ECHR, but recognised at [4] the inevitable tension between that objective with facilitating the free movement of data. That tension is not so evident in the domestic setting for which the Act provides, in particular, in the right of access to personal data with which this case was concerned. See paras 5.11 and 5.53 below.

In *Bodil Lindqvist*, C-101/01, 6 November 2003, the European Court of Justice found (at para 90) that the provisions of the Directive do not, in themselves, bring about a restriction which conflicts with the general principles of freedom of expression or other freedoms and rights, enshrined inter alia in Article 10 ECHR. The Court said it was for the national authorities and courts responsible for applying national legislation implementing the Directive to ensure a fair balance between the rights and interests in question.

C. Data Protection Act 1998

(1) Regime

5.07 The current Information Commissioner is Mr Richard Thomas. The Information Commissioner's website address is http://www.dataprotection. gov.uk and contains electronic versions of recent annual reports, the most recent being dated July 2003 for the year ending 31 March 2003 (available in hardcopy from HMSO). 'The Data Protection Act 1998—Legal Guidance', ISBN no 1 870466 23 3, December 2001, remains available in hardcopy, and is also accessible on the website. (The previous Information Commissioner, Elizabeth France, said in her foreword to the hardcopy Legal Guidance that as changes become necessary to the guidance as a result of decided cases the web version will be updated.) A selection of anonymised case studies continues to be published in the annual reports. There is not yet however a comprehensive record of tribunal decisions available on the website.

(2) Definitions—Data, Parties, Processing, Purposes

(a) **Data**

In *Campbell v MGN Ltd* the Court of Appeal accepted at [124] that the claimant would have had a claim under s 13 of the Act for the publication of the fact that she was a drug addict if s 32 did not exempt the newspaper publishers.
   5.09

(i) 'Equipment operating automatically in response to instructions given for that purpose'

In *Douglas v Hello! Ltd* [2003] 3 All ER 996 [230], [231] Lindsay J held that the *Hello!* defendants were each data controllers, the unauthorised pictures represented personal data and the publication of them in England was caught by DPA 1998. The act of publication itself formed part of the processing within the scope of the Act. The processing in *Douglas* involved the transmission of the pictures by ISDN line from California to London, their calling up on a screen in London, their transmission by ISDN line from London to Madrid, electronic touching up, transmission to the printers and the printing processes. There was also (unauthorised) publication of the pictures on a *Hello!* website.
   5.10

(ii) Relevant filing system—manual data

In *Durant v Financial Services Authority* [2003] EWCA Civ 1746 [50] the Court of Appeal concluded that a 'relevant filing system' is limited to a system in which the files are structured or referenced in such a way as clearly to indicate at the outset of the search whether specific information capable of amounting to personal data is held within the system; and which has, as part of its structure or referencing mechanism, a sufficiently sophisticated and detailed means of readily indicating whether and where an individual file's specific criteria about an individual can be located.
   5.11

(b) **Data controller and data processor**

In *Douglas v Hello! Ltd* [2003] EMLR 585 the Court of Appeal held that the argument that the sixth defendant, an American paparazzo, who transmitted the unauthorised photographs down an ISDN line to London fell within s 5(1)(b) of the DPA 1998 had a reasonable prospect of success and should not be struck out, reversing the decision of Laddie J at first instance. This was on the basis that it was at least arguable that the sixth defendant was a data controller for the purposes
   5.15

since he was on the pleaded case 'using equipment in the United Kingdom for processing [the] data otherwise than for the purposes of transit through the United Kingdom'. This interpretation assimilates liability for breaches of the statutory torts under the DPA 1998 to liability for causing the publication from abroad of a libel read in England.

5.17 In *Campbell v MGN Ltd* the Court of Appeal accepted at [76] that the newspaper publishers were a data controller. They also noted that the data controller tended to be equated with the editor, who had been personally responsible for the decisions taken in relation to the content of the articles complained of.

(f) Sensitive personal data

5.21 n41 See para 3.109 of this Supplement.

n42 The findings of the judge at first instance in *Campbell v MGN Ltd* as to what was, or may amount to, sensitive personal data were unaffected by the Court of Appeal's judgment.

In *Lord Ashcroft v (1) Attorney-General and (2) Department for International Development* [2002] EWHC 1122 (QB), Gray J held at [30] that it was at least arguable that a reference in a memorandum to the claimant's laundry arrangements would be understood to be a reference to the criminal offence of money-laundering, with the result that the memorandum in question could constitute sensitive personal data under DPA 1998, s 2(g).

In *R (Ellis) v Chief Constable of Essex Police* [2003] 2 FLR 566 [29] it was assumed that a scheme by the police to deter crime by publishing poster images of offenders would engage the DPA 1998, but it was considered that the position under the Act would be the same as under Article 8 itself.

(g) Processing

5.25 The Court of Appeal in *Campbell v MGN Ltd* concluded at [107] with reference to the Appellant newspaper and its editor as 'data controllers' within the terms of DPA 1998, that:

> . . . where the data controller is responsible for the publication of hard copies that reproduce data that has previously been processed by means of equipment operating automatically, the publication forms part of the processing and falls within the scope of the Act.

The Court added at [123] that 'the definition of processing is so wide that it embraces the relatively ephemeral operations that will normally be carried out by way of the day-to-day tasks, involving the use of electronic equipment, such as the laptop and the modern printing press, in translating information into the printed newspaper'.

(3) The Data Protection Principles

(a) First principle—processing to be fair and lawful

In *Campbell v MGN Ltd* [89] the Court of Appeal agreed with Morland J that un-   **5.32–5.42**
less it fell within the s 32 exemption, the newspaper was not in a position to satisfy the conditions imposed by the Act. The Court held at [122] that the
obligation of the data controller to inform the data subject that personal data had
been processed, and the rights of the data subject, for example to rectification, are
not appropriate for the data processing which will normally be an incident of journalism. The Court said at [123] that '[t]he speed at which [data processing has] to
be carried out if a newspaper is to publish news renders it impractical to comply
with many of the data processing principles and conditions in Schedules 2 and 3,
including the requirement that the data subject has given his consent to the processing.' The Court came to the conclusion at [133] that the claimant had not
consented, but that the public interest justified the publication of the article without her consent. As noted in the Supplement to para 5.05 above, there may be circumstances other than journalism, literature and the arts where similar
considerations apply. There are also cases involving literature and the arts where
the timescale is more prolonged than in the production of daily newspapers. In
such cases some or all of the considerations noted by the Court of Appeal may not
apply.

(i) The principle and its conditions

Personal data.   Consideration of whether data has been processed fairly and   **5.32**
lawfully in the context of publication by a media data controller will now only be
addressed once a court has come to the conclusion that the s 32 media exemption
does not apply on the facts of a particular case, given the Court of Appeal's decision in *Campbell v MGN Ltd* that the exemption applies before, after, and at the
moment of publication. However, it remains the position that if questions as to
lawfulness and/or fairness do arise, then information will not be obtained lawfully
if it is obtained in breach of confidence. Photographs (as happened in the
Campbell case) will not be obtained fairly if the subject has no opportunity of refusing consent. See also para 2.34 of the Main Work.

In *Douglas v Hello! Ltd* [2003] 3 All ER 996, Lindsay J found at [236] that the
obtaining of the unauthorised photographs and their processing, in particular
publication, was not fair. Further, no consent to the processing (including publication) of the unauthorised photographs was given by the data subjects, Mr and
Mrs Douglas: [237]. He also found at [238] that whilst the *Hello!* defendants did
have a legitimate interest for the purposes of DPA 1998, Sch 2 para 6, namely the
publication of their magazine to include coverage of the Douglas' wedding, the
particular processing they had carried out in pursuit of that interest was

illegitimate since it was unwarranted by reason of prejudice to the rights of the data subjects. Lindsay J held that a finding of prejudice under this provision did not require a general balance between freedom of expression and rights to privacy or confidence, but rather a consideration simply of whether something more than trivial prejudice had arisen to the data subjects' legal rights.

5.34 **Sensitive personal data.** The judge's finding in *Campbell* at first instance that the requirements of the first principle are cumulative was unaffected by the Court of Appeal's judgment.

(d) Sixth principle—processing in accordance with rights of data subjects

(i) Section 7—right of access

5.53 As noted in the Main Work, DPA, ss 7(9) and 15(1) give the High Court or County Court discretion to order a data controller to comply with a data access request if he has failed to do so in compliance with the Act. Although Parliament clearly intended that there should be a discretion, by using the expression 'may order' as opposed to 'must order' in s 7(9), it is submitted that a court should decline to make such an order only in exceptional circumstances, where the making of the request amounts to an abuse of process. Any lower threshold for denying an applicant his statutory privacy right to personal information held or processed about him would be wrong in principle. In *P v Wozencroft* [2002] 2 FLR 1118, Wilson J declined to make an order for disclosure of documents pursuant to s 7, on the basis of evidence before him to the effect that the documents being sought had never existed. He also, in his discretion under s 14, declined rectification of information held by the data controller, on the basis that the rectification sought (an attempt to amend an opposing party's expert report in previous concluded litigation) was an abuse of the Court's process.

In *Durant v Financial Services Authority* the Court at first instance declined to make an order under s 7 on the basis that it found that the data controller, the FSA, had in fact complied with the request made of it. However, the Court also held that had it come to the contrary conclusion, that the FSA had failed to comply with the data access request made of it, it would still in its discretion have declined to make an order. The reasons given were, first, that the information being sought (about himself) could be of no practical value to the applicant. Secondly, the purpose of DPA 1998 is to ensure that records of an inaccurate nature are not kept about an individual, rather than to fuel a separate collateral argument the applicant has with the data controller or another third party (in that case, Barclays Bank). And, thirdly, the FSA had acted at all times in good faith. The Court of Appeal took a different approach from the judge below. It held that the data requested by the applicant did not constitute 'personal data' within the meaning of s 1(1) DPA and he was therefore not entitled to access it under s 7. Being named in the data requested (even though this might be a practical requirement) did not give an automatic right of access. To qualify, the data had to concern the individual who requested it in the sense of affecting his privacy, it had to be biographical in a significant sense and have the putative data subject as its focus: [2003] EWCA Civ 1746 [27]–[28]. Furthermore, it held at [60]–[61] that the court's function under s 7(9) DPA was not to 'second guess' decisions of data-controllers. The correct degree of review was 'anxious scrutiny.' Where access to the data might disclose the identity of another individual the court should be entitled to ask what legitimate interest the data subject had in obtaining that information, subject to the discretion of the court to order access to a redacted version of the data.

Cuttings service.   *Lord Ashcroft v (1) Attorney-General and (2) Department For*   **5.58**
International Development now provides an instance where a claimant 'energetically pursued' personal data access requests under s 7, DPA and, having thereby obtained 'disclosure' of documents, applied successfully to amend his pleaded case on the basis of documents so obtained: [2002] EWHC 1122 (QB), [10], [11]. See also the discussion of *P v Wozencroft* and *Durant v Financial Services Authority* above in this Supplement to para 5.53.

(e) Seventh principle—security (f) Eighth principle—transfer outside EEA

Whilst the disclosure of data may be evidence of a breach of the obligations as to se-   **5.63–5.64**
curity and/or transfer, the conclusion that the seventh and/or eighth principles have been breached if disclosure has occurred is not automatic. In such circumstances a court may not permit a free-standing claim based on alleged breach of the seventh and/or eighth principles when the crux of a claimant's complaint concerns disclosures that offend the Act's other substantive provisions: *Lord Ashcroft v (1) Attorney-General and (2) Department For International Development* at [27], [35].

In the context of transfer of data between Member States the European Court of Justice found in *Bodil Lindqvist*, C-101/01, 6 November 2003 that the uploading of personal data by an individual from her computer to an internet host (not in the same country), thus making that data available on the internet generally, was not in itself a transfer of data to a third country within the meaning of Article 25 of the Directive.

(4) Further Rights of Data Subjects

(a) Section 13—compensation

(i) Section 13

In *Lord Ashcroft v (1) Attorney-General and (2) Department For International*   **5.66**

Development Gray J at [29] interpreted the 1998 Act as containing a free-standing duty on data controllers to comply with the data protection principles, breach of which sounds in damages under s 13, as does breach of any of the other requirements of the Act. By contrast, he found at [26] that the Data Protection Act 1984 conferred a private law right to damages only by its s 23 in respect of the alleged disclosure of documents in that case. Any other breach of the 1984 Act or its principles was found to be a matter for the Information Commissioner, rather than for a damages claim through the courts. The action concerned the leak of personal information about Lord Ashcroft from government files. Compare *Craxi (No 2) v Italy*, Application no 25337/94, judgment of 17 July 2003, in which it was held that the leak of personal information from court files was a breach of Article 8 by the State, as was the subsequent failure to hold an effective investigation: [72]–[76]. See further the Supplement to paras 1.76 above 6.40, 12.25, and 12.31 below.

n147 The Court of Appeal in *Campbell v MGN Ltd* found the Appellant newspaper to be protected by the s 32 exemption in any event. It follows that the data controller cannot, in the language of s 13 of the Act, have been in 'contravention . . . of any of the requirements of the Act. . .', because the requirements do not *ex hypothesi* apply to the data controller in question, by virtue of the s 32 exemption. See the Supplement to paras 5.32–5.42 above.

In *Douglas v Hello! Ltd* [2003] 3 All ER 996, Lindsay J found that although the Douglases had established claims to compensation under s 13, because there had been a breach of the Act, the DPA claim did not add a separate route to recovery for damage or distress beyond a nominal award. That is because the judge could not see how it could reasonably be said with reference to the wording of s 13 that the damage and distress occasioned to the Douglases was '. . . by reason of any contravention . . . of [the] Act'. So too in *R (Ellis) v Chief Constable of Essex Police* [2003] 2 FLR 566 the Court held that a claim under the DPA 1998 added nothing to the claim under Article 8: see further para 6.40 of the Main Work and the Supplement thereto.

(ii) 'Careless falsehood'

5.69 n149 Since the Court of Appeal in *Campbell v MGN Ltd* reversed Morland J's finding for the claimant on liability, the award at first instance in her favour and valued at £3,500 is of historic interest only. However, the Court of Appeal did confirm at [139] that it would have been open to the judge to consider an award of aggravated damages, had his finding in her favour otherwise been valid. The award in *Douglas v Hello! Ltd* [2003] 3 All ER 996 in relation to an established breach of DPA 1998 was for nominal damages only in a case where there was a parallel claim for damage and distress suffered by reason of a breach of confidence: see the Supplement to para 5.66 n147 above.

(b) Section 14 —rectification, blocking, erasure, destruction

See the Supplement to paras 5.32–5.42 above for the inappropriateness of these **5.70** remedies to journalism.

(5) Media Exemptions and Defences

(a) Section 32(1) to (3)—prior restraint

(ii) No prior restraint

The Court of Appeal's decision in *Campbell v MGN Ltd* [2003] QB 633 has fun- **5.80** damentally altered the position stated in this paragraph. The Court of Appeal held at [120], [121] and [128]–[131] that DPA 1998 subsections 32(1)–(3) apply to provide an exemption both before and after publication. The exemption applies in relation to data, and information which is published remains data as defined by the Act. This part of the judgment reversed Morland J's decision at first instance. For a discussion of the reasons for, and the implications of, this conclusion see the Supplement to paras 5.05 and 5.32–5.34 above. On the facts in *Campbell*, the Court of Appeal found that the s 32 exemption had been made out by the news-paper:

(1) It was conceded (at [133]) that the processing in question had been under-taken with a view to the publication by the newspaper and its editor of jour-nalistic material, which satisfied s 32(1)(a);

(2) The Court of Appeal held at [132]–[133] and [137] that the publication was 'a journalistic package that it was reasonable to publish in the public inter-est'—the editor had given evidence of his belief to such effect to the trial judge, which he had accepted as truthful—and so s 32(1)(b) was satisfied. The reasons identified for the public interest were (i) it appeared that the claimant had been committing offences of possessing Class A drugs, (ii) as a role model to young people, she had held herself out as someone who re-mained immune from drugs in an industry where drug abuse was notoriously common, and (iii) she had frequently made references to her private life in many interviews with the media. It had been conceded (at [36] and [38]) that by mendaciously asserting to the media that she did not take drugs, she had rendered it legitimate for the media to put the record straight by publishing the bald fact that she was receiving treatment;

(3) Similarly, the Court accepted at [137] that the editor reasonably believed that in all the circumstances compliance with the Act was incompatible with the special purposes, which satisfied s 32(1)(c). On the facts, the newspaper had attempted to obtain the claimant's consent to its proposed publication (ie consent to processing) but the claimant had refused: see [133]. Thus, whilst the public interest justified publication by the newspaper, it knew it was un-able to comply with the Act without Ms Campbell's consent to publication.

In these circumstances, its belief that compliance with the Act was incompatible with its journalistic pursuit was correct as well as reasonable: see [137].

(iv) Reasonable belief that publication would be in the public interest

5.83 See the Supplement to para 5.80 above.

Where the media would seek to justify a publication on the basis that naming a wrongdoer will shame him or her into desisting from his or her wrongful conduct, similar concerns will arise as those considered in *R (Ellis) v Chief Constable of Essex Police* [2003] 2 FLR 566 (that publicity may make rehabilitation more difficult, and that family members may suffer adverse consequences): see the Supplement to para 2.14 above.

5.84 n188 In *Douglas v Hello! Ltd* [2003] 3 All ER 996, Lindsay J found (at [231]) that the s 32 exemption did not apply since there was no credible evidence that the *Hello!* defendants believed publication of the disputed photographs would be in the public interest and there was no room anyway for any conclusion that publication could reasonably be regarded as in the public interest.

(v) Reasonable belief that compliance with the principles and the data subject's rights is incompatible with the special purposes

5.85 See the Supplement to para 5.80 above.

(a) Section 32(4) and (5)—stay

5.86 In *Campbell v MGN Ltd* the Court of Appeal confirmed at [116] that DPA 1998 ss 32(4) and 32(5) are purely procedural. Further, the stay is to subsist unless and until either the data controller's claim to a stay is withdrawn or the Information Commissioner determines the claim is not valid. It is to be inferred that if publication takes place before the Commissioner has ruled on the claim to a stay then the stay ceases to be effective: see [116].

(c) The Data Protection (Processing of Sensitive Personal Data) Order 2000

(iii) The substantial public interest

5.90 Morland J's finding in *Campbell v MGN Ltd* at first instance, that disclosure of the claimant's therapy at Narcotics Anonymous was not in the *substantial* public interest, has now been overtaken by the Court of Appeal's finding.

(d) DPA 1998, Schedule 2, paragraph 6(1)

5.95 In *Douglas v Hello! Ltd* [2003] 3 All ER 996 at [238] Lindsay J found the *Hello!* defendants to have a legitimate interest within DPA 1998, Sch 2 para 6, namely the publication of their magazine to include coverage of the Douglas' wedding. But see further the Supplement to para 5.32 above for his explanation as to why on the facts of that case the *Hello!* defendants were not protected.

(6) CCTV Surveillance

n206 See the Supplement to paras 1.69 and 2.35 above for discussion of the **5.99** ECtHR judgment in *Peck v UK* (2003) 36 EHRR 41.

6

PRIVACY AND CONFIDENTIALITY

A. Introduction

In *Campbell v MGN Ltd* [2003] QB 633, [42]–[43], [70] the Court of Appeal said that the Human Rights Act has had a significant impact on the law of confidentiality, and that when considering what information is confidential the Courts must have regard to the Article 8 right to respect for private and family life, and to the importance of freedom of expression. For a review of the authorities on breach   **6.02** of confidence in the context of privacy, see *Hosking v Runting* (High Court of New Zealand, 30 May 2003) and the Supplement to paras 4.12–4.14 above.

6.03 In *Campbell v MGN Ltd* at [70] the Court of Appeal said that where information relates to an aspect of an individual's private life which he does not choose to make public, the unjustifiable publication of such information would be better described as a breach of privacy than a breach of confidence. In *Wainwright v Home Office* [2003] 3 WLR 1137, [30] the House of Lords confirmed that English law does not recognise a general tort of invasion of privacy but left open for another day the question of whether the old action for breach of confidence should be extended and possibly renamed.

nn11, 12 For discussion of situations where there may be a breach of privacy but not a breach of confidence, see Main Work paras 4.15–4.18 and 6.157. *Campbell v MGN Ltd* provides a further example: see the Supplement to para 6.157 below.

B. The Cause of Action for Breach of Confidence: an Overview

(1) Origins and Development

6.06 n17 See Lindsay J's characterisation of *Prince Albert v Strange* in his judgment following the trial of the issue of liability in *Douglas v Hello! Ltd* [2003] 3 All ER 996, at [181], as 'a case as to personal confidence but in which authorities on commercial confidence are cited'.

(2) Juridical Bases

(c) Tort or *sui generis*

6.10 *Clerk & Lindsell on Torts* (18th edn) gives support to characterising a claim in confidence as a tort: paras 1.01, 1.02, 1.12 and 1.34. The question may be of practical importance in considering the applicable law under the Private International Law (Miscellaneous Provisions) Act 1995, s 11. If it is not a tort, *Dicey & Morris* suggest that the applicable law is the law of the country where enrichment occurs: *The Conflict of Laws* (13th edn) para 34-009 (9). This would be likely to raise difficult questions, and lead to multiple applicable laws in cases where individuals in different jurisdictions are involved. See the Supplement to para 4.49 above.

(3) Essential Elements of the Cause of Action

6.11 n32 The approach of the Court of Appeal in *A v B plc* [2003] QB 195 could be thought to cast doubt on whether the *Coco v Clark* analysis remains apposite in cases concerned with personal information. The Court analysed the requirements of a valid confidence claim in respect of information of this nature without reference to *Coco v Clark*. See further the Supplement to para 6.12 below.

(a) Information having the quality of confidence

6.12 n34 Recent authorities have taken approaches to the definition of what is confidential in character which differ from the approach outlined in the Main Work. In *A v B plc* [2003] QB 195 the Court of Appeal observed that authorities which relate to the action for breach of confidence before the Human Rights Act came into force are 'largely of historic interest only': [9]. It held that a claim in confidence may now lie when 'there is an interest of a private nature which the claimant wishes to protect . . . worthy of protection': [11](vii).

In *Campbell v MGN Ltd* the Court of Appeal observed at [70] that

> the development of the law of confidentiality since the Human Rights Act 1998 came into force has seen information described as 'confidential' not where it has been confided by one person to another, but where it relates to an aspect of an individual's private life which he does not choose to make public.

The Court also approved the trial judge's application of the test of whether disclosure of the information at issue would be highly offensive to a reasonable person of ordinary sensibilities (the 'offensiveness' test).

In *Douglas v Hello! Ltd*, Lindsay J applied the conventional *Coco v Clark* approach (see Main Work at para 6.11). However, he considered that the first element demanded no more than the information be inaccessible: see [182]–[183] and [189]. He regarded it as:

> important to note . . . that the citation from Lord Greene MR [in *Coco v A N Clark (Engineers) Ltd* [1969] RPC 41, 47] as to the information having to have 'the necessary quality of confidence about it' is a citation that stops mid-sentence. Lord Greene MR's sentence in full read (with emphasis added): 'The information, to be confidential must, I apprehend, apart from contract, have the necessary quality of confidence about it, *namely, it must not be something which is public property and public knowledge*'.

Lindsay J went on to derive from this that:

> The 'necessary quality of confidence' which Megarry J contemplated, by his adoption of Lord Greene MR's dictum, *was and was only therefore a quality of that particular kind*. I mention this as there is a suspicion that in some later cases the phrase 'necessary quality of confidence' has been regarded as including factors other than such as Lord Greene MR had had in mind. Instead, at the point at which Megarry J was considering it . . . *the question*. . . . *is whether the information has 'the basic attribute of inaccessibility'*. (emphasis added)

In relation to this point, see further para 6.89ff of the Main Work and the Supplement to para 6.90 below.

It appears from Lindsay J's judgment at [193] that he regarded other factors pertaining to the quality of the information at issue, such as those discussed in paras 6.82–6.88 of the Main Work and the Supplement thereto below as bearing only on the question of whether relief, and if so what relief, should be granted in a particular case. He seems to have regarded the 'offensiveness' test as playing the same role. See the discussion and comments in this Supplement to paras 6.42 and 6.148 below.

n35 See also *Campbell v MGN Ltd* at [51], agreeing that usually it will be obvious whether there is a private interest worthy of protection.

6.13 The Court of Appeal in *Campbell v MGN Ltd* took a different approach from that of Morland J cited in the last sentence of this paragraph. The Court observed that the existence of inaccuracies in the additional information of which complaint was made strengthened their conclusion that disclosure of that information was 'in its context, of insufficient importance to shock the conscience and justify the intervention of the court': see [56]–[57].

(4) The Position of Third Parties

(a) Those who acquire information from a confidant or by some other means

6.18 n55 The Court of Appeal in *Campbell v MGN Ltd* held at [66]–[70] that where the publication of personal as opposed to commercial information is concerned, it is not necessary to prove dishonesty against the third party:

> The suggestion that complex tests of the mental state of the publisher have to be satisfied before breach of confidence can be made out in respect of publication of information which violates the right of enjoyment of private or family life is not acceptable.

(b) Those on notice of injunctions against others

6.19 Contempt of court of the kind described in the last sentence of this paragraph can only be committed by the destruction of confidentiality protected by an interim injunction, as opposed to a final order. See the Supplement to para 6.136 below.

D. Types of Information Protected in Confidence

(3) Personal Information Contrasted with Other Types of Information

(a) Distinguishing personal from commercial information

6.37 Lindsay J distinguished the commercial and personal claims of the claimants to confidentiality in *Douglas v Hello! Ltd.* He regarded the Douglases' claim primarily as a traditional commercial confidentiality or trade secret case, and not as a privacy complaint. He treated their wedding as 'a commercial entity attracting such aspects of the law of confidence as can be deployed to protect trade secrets' (see [195]ff) and information personal to the claimants about it as such a trade secret, that is, as a valuable, saleable commodity. On this basis, he found that the first condition required for a cause of action for breach of confidence, as he construed it, was satisfied (see the Supplement to para 6.11 n32 above).

Lindsay J also found that the *Hello!* defendants had intruded into the claimants' private lives without their consent and without justification: see [205]. However, he regarded the invasion of the privacy as material only to the application of s 12 of the Human Rights Act and to whether the claimants ought to be granted substantive relief: see [202].

In taking this approach, Lindsay J recognised (at [196]) that it 'may lead to a distinction between the circumstances in which equity affords protection to those who seek to manage their publicity as part of their trade or profession and whose private life is a valuable commodity and those whose is not' but went on to say, 'I am untroubled by that; the law which protects individual confidences and a law of privacy may protect the latter class and provide no reason to diminish protection for the former.' He went on to conclude at [227] that:

> In my judgment, and first regarding the Claimants' case as one of either commercial confidence or of a hybrid kind in which, by reason of it having become a commodity, elements that would otherwise have been merely private became commercial, I find the *Hello!* Defendants to have acted unconscionably and that, by reason of breach of confidence, they are liable to all three Claimants to the extent of the detriment which was thereby caused to the Claimant respectively.

(b) Distinguishing personal from government information

The approach of the court in *Venables v News Group Newspapers Ltd* and *A v B plc* **6.40** (paras 6.14–6.16 of the Main Work) means that provided the information at issue is recognisably of a confidential character it may not be necessary for a claimant, suing the media in respect of the publication of information disclosed to it by a public body, to establish that the public body owed him a private law duty of confidence.

n105 The existence of a duty on the State to protect from misuse personal information which the State has acquired is bolstered by the Strasbourg authorities. In *Peck v UK* (2003) 36 EHRR 41, the ECtHR noted at [59] that:

> . . . in both the *Rotaru* and *Amann* judgments (to which the *PG and JH* [*v UK*, Application 44787/98, Judgment of 25 September 2001] judgment referred), the compilation of data by security services on particular individuals even without the

use of covert surveillance methods constituted an interference with the applicants' privates lives (*Rotaru v Romania* [[2000] 8 BHRC 449] [43]–[44], and *Amann v Switzerland* [(2000) 30 EHRR 843] [65]–[67]).

In *Craxi (No 2) v Italy*, Application no 25337/94, judgment of 17 July 2003, [73] and [76], it was held that where unpublished personal information held in a Court Registry was leaked to the press there was a breach by the State of its obligation to secure the right to respect for private life and correspondence. It was further held that in the case of such a leak it is the obligation of the State to carry out effective inquiries to rectify the matter to the extent possible: [74]–[75]. See further the Supplement to paras 1.76 above and 12.25 and 12.31 below. For proceedings brought on a similar basis (ie under Article 8 and under the Data Protection Act 1998) in respect of documents leaked from a Ministry see *Lord Ashcroft v (1) Attorney-General and (2) Department for International Development* [2002] EWHC 1122 (QB).

However, some information obtained by Government is required or authorised to be made available on public records or registers, such as the electoral roll or registers of marriages. For a discussion of how personal information of this kind should be treated by the law of confidence, see para 6.102 of this Supplement below.

n110 In *Peck v UK*, the ECtHR held unanimously that the applicant's rights under Article 8 had been violated, holding at [87] as follows:

> . . . the Court considers that the disclosures by the Council of the CCTV material in the 'CCTV News' and to the 'Yellow Advertiser', Anglia Television and to the BBC were not accompanied by sufficient safeguards to prevent disclosure inconsistent with the guarantees of respect for the applicant's private life contained in Article 8 of the Convention. As such, the disclosure constituted a disproportionate and therefore unjustified interference with his private life and a violation of Article 8 of the Convention.

The rationale of the decision was, at [85], that:

> the Court does not find that, in the circumstances of this case, there were relevant or sufficient reasons which would justify the direct disclosure by the Council to the public of stills from the footage in its own publication 'CCTV News' without the Council obtaining the applicant's consent or masking his identity, or which would justify its disclosures to the media without the Council taking steps to ensure so far as possible that such masking would be effected by the media. The crime prevention objective and context of the disclosures demanded particular scrutiny and care in these respects in the present case.

See also *Perry v UK*, Application no 63737/00, judgment of 17 July 2003, where use of an image obtained covertly by the police for the purposes of identification was held to be a breach of Article 8 because the provisions of the applicable Code under PACE had not been applied. See the Supplement to para 3.21 above.

n111 Public bodies can owe obligations of confidentiality to individuals distinct from their general duty to act in good faith in the execution of their duties. In *R v Inland Revenue Commissioners, ex p National Federation of Self Employed and Small Businesses Ltd* [1982] AC 617, 654 Lord Scarman recognised the existence of a duty of fairness owed to the general body of taxpayers by the Inland Revenue and, co-existing with it, the specific duty of confidence owed to each individual taxpayer.

In *Re W (Care Proceedings; Disclosure)* [2003] 2 FLR 1023 a local authority was permitted by the Court to disclose to other parties to care proceedings, and in particular to the mother, a sensitive piece of confidential information received from the police, subject to precautions against identification of an informant, and against prejudicing a police enquiry.

(4) Classes of Personal Information Which May be Protected as Confidential

n116 The Court of Appeal has now expressly approved the following as, at least, **6.42** a useful practical test in many circumstances of what personal information or conduct is private and worthy of protection: 'whether disclosure or observation of the information or conduct would be highly offensive to a reasonable person of ordinary sensibilities': see *Campbell v MGN Ltd* [48]–[51]. Morland J had adopted that test at first instance, drawing it from dicta of Gleeson CJ in *Australian Broadcasting Corporation v Lenah Game Meats Pty Ltd* [2001] HCA 63, [42], which appeared to have at least the implicit approval of the Court of Appeal in *A v B plc* [2003] QB 195 at [11(vii)]. The origins of the test lie further back, in the work of the US jurist Dean Prosser.

In approving the application of this test by the trial judge in *Campbell,* the Court of Appeal accepted that it embraced both the question of whether information was private and also the question of the degree of its significance but observed that 'we do not consider that the test is any the worse for that'. The court did not consider very meaningful any attempt to distinguish between what is 'offensive' and 'highly offensive', but some guidance on the degree of offence that is required to satisfy the test may be gleaned from the Court of Appeal's findings at [54] and [56], the latter of which was that the disclosure complained of in *Campbell* was not 'of sufficient significance to shock the conscience and justify the intervention of the court'.

However, Lindsay J in *Douglas v Hello! Ltd* at [188]–[193] considered that it could not have been the intention of the Court of Appeal in *Campbell* to use the *Lenah Game Meats* test, 'as a yardstick appropriate for judging whether the first *Coco* test was satisfied'. He believed that Gleeson CJ at [190]–[191] was using the 'offensiveness' yardstick only in the context of the new tort of privacy being advanced in that case, and not in connection with traditional, equitable rights of confidence. He therefore declined to apply it. Nevertheless, the relevant paragraphs from the judgment of Gleeson CJ ([34]–[35]) can be read as indicating that the learned Chief Justice was using the yardstick not in the context of privacy, but the law of confidence as set forth by Laws J in *Hellewell v Chief Constable of Derbyshire* [1995] 1 WLR 804, 807. As regards Lindsay J's view, see also the Supplement to para 6.12 n34 above.

(a) Information about health and medical treatment

(i) Scope

6.44 The jurisprudence of the ECtHR, as summarised in *Peck v UK* at [78], makes clear that the privacy of certain information about health lies at the heart of the protection designed to be afforded by Article 8:

> The Court noted [in *Z v Finland* (1997) EHRR 371] that the protection of personal data was of fundamental importance to a person's enjoyment of his or her right to respect for private life and that the domestic law must therefore afford appropriate safeguards to prevent any such disclosure as may be inconsistent with the guarantees in Article 8 of the Convention. In so finding, the Court referred, *mutatis mutandis*, to Articles 3 § 2 (c), 5, 6 and 9 of the Convention for the Protection of Individuals with Regard to Automatic Processing of Personal Data (European Treaty Series no. 108, Strasbourg, 1981). It went on to find that the above considerations were 'especially valid' as regards the protection of the confidentiality of information about a person's HIV status, noting that the interests in protecting the confidentiality of such information weighed heavily in the balance in determining whether the interference was proportionate to the legitimate aim pursued. Such interference could not be compatible with Article 8 of the Convention unless it was justified by an overriding requirement in the public interest.

It may also be observed that where the Court is required by HRA, s 12(4) to have regard to the PCC Code, a claimant will be able to rely on the fact that clause 3 (Privacy) not only substantially repeats the wording of Article 8, but expressly refers to 'health' as a private matter which a person is entitled to have respected by the press.

In *Lady Archer v Williams* [2003] FSR 869 the confidentiality of medical information was conceded (see paras [34]–[35]) and damages were awarded for disclosure of information about cosmetic surgery (see [74]–[75]).

n121 See also *Mersey Care NHS Trust v Ackroyd* [2003] FSR 820.

6.45 The Court of Appeal in *Campbell v MGN Ltd* took a different view from Morland J on this point. It did not consider 'that the information that Miss Campbell was receiving therapy from Narcotics Anonymous was to be equated with disclosure of clinical details of medical treatment': see [48]. Applying the test referred to at the Supplement to para 6.42 above, the Court held at [54] that:

... we do not consider that a reasonable person of ordinary sensibilities, on reading that Miss Campbell was a drug addict, would find it highly offensive, or even offensive, that the *Mirror* also disclosed that she was attending meetings of Narcotics Anonymous.

However, this was said in the context of the publishers having conceded that 'the information, were it not for the lies and the need to correct public posturing, would plainly be confidential': [37], [38]. It was the Court's view that the disclosures complained of were 'peripheral' in this context that led it to conclude that the intervention of the Court was not justified: [56], [58].

n122 See now the Court of Appeal's judgment in *Campbell v MGN Ltd* at [48], [53] and [54].

(ii) Limitations

For a discussion of whether disclosure of anonymised data can ever be a breach of confidence, see the Supplement to para 6.144 below. **6.46**

(b) Information about sexual life

(i) Scope

The confidentiality of information relating to the claimant's marital sexual relations was conceded in *Lady Archer v Williams* [2003] FSR 869. So was the claimant's right to claim confidentiality in respect of the sexual relationships of any of her children. See ibid [34]–[35]. As to this last point see the Supplement to para 6.65 below. **6.47**

(ii) Limitations

Even if details of a sexual relationship are private and confidential it may not follow that the mere fact of the sexual relationship is confidential: see the discussion of the fact/detail distinction at paras 6.85–6.87 of the Main Work. In any case it does not follow that other information about the relationship, of a less intimate nature, is confidential: see further the Supplement to para 6.57 below. **6.49**

(c) Information about appearance

(i) Scope

In *Douglas v Hello! Ltd* Lindsay J held, at [197], that: **6.51**

photographic representation of the wedding reception . . . had the quality of confidence about it. Of course, the general appearance of both Mr Douglas and Miss Zeta-Jones was no secret; what they looked like was well known to the public. But that does not deny the quality of commercial confidentiality to what they looked like on the exceptional occasion of their wedding.

In relation to information about an individual's appearance, see also the Supplement to para 6.62 below.

(ii) Limitations

6.52 In *Campbell v MGN Ltd* the Court of Appeal held that the publication of photographs showing the claimant in the street was not a breach of confidence. The photographs 'did not convey any information that was confidential': [33]. First instance courts in England and New Zealand have also rejected claims in confidence in respect of the publication of photographs of individuals in the street: *MGN Ltd v Attard* (Connell J, 19 October 2001); *Hosking v Runting* (High Court of New Zealand, 30 May 2003).

It does not necessarily follow, however, that the publication of photographs of individuals in street scenes can never found a claim in confidence. In *Campbell* it was the captions which told the story. They explained that the photographs showed the claimant leaving a therapy session. Publication of that information was not a breach of confidence because it was insufficiently offensive and protected by a public interest justification. It remains open to argument that a photograph which by itself tells the reader something secret and highly sensitive, for instance about a claimant's medical condition, conveys confidential information, even if taken in the street. A possible example is a photograph showing a person stepping into the street in obvious distress under a sign identifying the location as a cancer clinic. Each case will fall to be considered on its own facts: cf *Bradley v Wingnut Films* [1993] 1 NZLR 415, 424.

Moreover, since the Court of Appeal's decision in *Campbell*, the ECtHR has ruled in *Peck v UK* that in providing to the media the CCTV footage featuring the applicant attempting to commit suicide in a public place without imposing sufficient restrictions on the disclosure of his identity, Brentwood Borough Council violated his rights under Article 8: see the Supplement to para 6.40, n110 above. The *Peck* case shows that even 'public' information may fall within the scope of 'private life' under Article 8 if recorded in permanent form, and that the disclosure of such a record by a public authority may amount to an unjustified interference with the rights under Article 8(1). Media organisations may not in general be public authorities under the Human Rights Act, but there are signs that the public/private distinction may be breaking down in this context also (see Main Work 1.80–1.84). It may therefore be open to argument that the English law of confidence/privacy must now, in appropriate circumstances, accommodate private law claims against the media in respect of the disclosure of information about conduct which is public in the sense that it occurs in a public place.

In *Campbell v MGN Ltd* the claimant did not pursue any claim in respect of the taking (as opposed to the publication) of the photographs; as the Court noted at

[54]: 'The reader might have found it offensive that what were obviously covert photographs had been taken of her, but that, of itself, is not relied on as a ground for legal complaint.' The Court here appears to be recognising that the mere taking of a photograph conveying information which is not secret might arguably be protected by a claim in privacy rather than confidence.

For discussion of photographs taken without consent, see paras 2.28–2.29 and 2.34 of the Main Work.

(d) Other information about identity

(i) Scope

In *X and Y v News Group Newspapers and MGN Ltd* [2003] FSR 850 Butler-Sloss **6.54** P made *contra mundum* orders to preserve the secrecy of information likely to lead to the identification and the disclosure of the whereabouts of the claimants, the child-killer Mary Bell and her daughter, notwithstanding that their Article 2 rights were unlikely to be affected by the refusal of the injunctions. The injunction was grounded in the law of confidence but, significantly, unlike in *Venables*, the Court found that the likely effect on Mary Bell's Article 8 rights alone justified the relief sought. The Article 8 rights specifically engaged were the protection granted to a person's physical and psychological integrity (*X v Netherlands* (1985) 8 EHRR 235, [22]) and the right to personal development and to establish and develop relationships with other human beings and the outside world (*Botta v Italy* (1998) 26 EHRR 241 and *Bensaid v UK* (2001) 33 EHRR 10): see *X and Y* at [20]. Y, Mary Bell's daughter, was considered to have grounds of independent complaint under Article 8, but Butler-Sloss P did not decide the issue of whether or not to extend the protection to Y on those grounds. The injunction was extended to Y because unmasking her would result in the identification of her mother: see [46]–[50]. The judge emphasised that the decision was not a charter for (*contra mundum*) orders benefiting convicted criminals: see [59]. Although that is undoubtedly true, the decision is important because of the recognition accorded to Article 8 rights in this sphere. See also the Supplement to para 6.62 below.

Information about a person's address and whereabouts is more likely to be regarded as confidential if the publication of it is likely to lead to harm or harassment. For example, the House of Commons has held that it is a contempt of the House to harass politicians: *Daily Graphic* case, HC 27 (1956–57): publication of a newspaper article inviting readers to telephone a member at his home to express their view about a question which he had tabled. In *R v Felixstowe JJ, ex p Leigh* [1987] 1 All ER 551, 561d it was held that the public are entitled to know names, but not addresses, of justices; that a loss of privacy to that extent is an incident of office. See *R (Al-Pawwaz) v Brixton Prison Governor* [2002] 2 WLR 101 [82]–[86] for identification of witnesses.

Another form of harm relates to the possible commercial exploitation of the address for soliciting business: see para 6.71 n209 of the Main Work and restraint of trade cases (where the concern is for the former employer), *Bullivant v Ellis* [1987] ICR 464, 474 and *Robb v Green* [1895] 2 QB 1, 18–19.

(e) Information about private acts

(i) Scope

6.56 When does a private act or event become a public act or event? In *Douglas v Hello! Ltd* [2001] QB 967, 995, Brooke LJ expressed the view that the claimants 'did not choose to have a private wedding attended by a few members of their family and a few friends in the normal sense of the words "private wedding"'. Having heard the evidence at trial, Lindsay J at [69] took a different view:

> I would be uneasy at characterising a wedding as not private simply on the basis of numbers, especially where the means of the parties were so ample that even a lavish wedding for 350–360 would not make real inroads, where the couple were popular enough to have many friends and where elaborate security arrangements were in place. But, amongst the evidence which I have had but which was not available to the Court of Appeal, is not only Miss Martel Levinson's as to security arrangements and the guest list itself but also Mr Douglas' which includes:—
>
> > 'Out of our guest list, approximately 125 of our guests were family members . . . If we had invited all the members of our families that we had wanted to then we would have needed a considerably larger venue or would not have been able to invite any of our friends.'
>
> It was, in my judgment, a private wedding.

(ii) Limitations

6.57 If private acts become general knowledge then the 'public domain' doctrine may mean that they can no longer be considered private and confidential: Main Work para 6.89. However, a limited degree of public knowledge may not satisfy the public domain doctrine, and confidentiality in personal information can survive even extensive publicity: see Main Work paras 6.90–6.93, 6.98. But this begs the difficult question of whether an act is private and confidential in the first place. If conduct is carried on in public with no attempt to keep it from prying eyes then it may not fall within the scope of what is 'private', whatever the nature of the conduct: see, as regards Article 8 of the Convention, *Peck v UK* at [65]–[66] and, as regards confidentiality, the discussion at paras 6.76–6.77 of the Main Work. A person's naked appearance may be considered a personal and private matter, but if he chooses to expose his body by streaking at a public sporting event then images and other information about this would surely be outside the scope of the law of confidence or privacy. More prosaically, although information about personal relationships may, obviously, be confidential it is hard to believe the courts would hold that one single person openly 'going out' with another single person was entitled to claim that the mere information that this was so was, without more, private and confidential information.

(f) Information about knowledge of or involvement in crime

(i) Scope

In *Rowe v Fryers* [2003] 1 WLR 1952, at [35] Scott Baker LJ (with the agreement **6.58** of Wilson J) held:

> It is, in my judgment, clear beyond doubt that confidentiality attaches to what is said to the police in the course of a criminal investigation and that this applies whether the person giving the information is a suspect who is interviewed under caution or merely a potential witness. For my part I cannot see any distinction in principle.

n161 See also *Woolgar v Chief Constable of Sussex Police* [2000] 1 WLR 25 and *R (Green) v Police Complaints Authority* [2002] UKHRR 985. For a more detailed discussion of private and public duties of confidence owed by the police and other public bodies with investigatory functions in respect of information provided to them by witnesses in the course of investigations, see para 6.40 of the Main Work and the Supplement to that para above.

n171 In *Mahon v Rahn (No 2)* [2000] 1 WLR 2151 at [187], Brooke LJ inter- **6.59** preted the House of Lords' decision in the *Taylor* case as supporting the existence of an implied undertaking at common law in respect of used material in criminal proceedings:

> Although I ruled at first instance that [the relevant document's] publication in court made no difference, the Court of Appeal expressly overruled me as a free-standing ground of its decision . . . The House of Lords in *Taylor v Director of the Serious Fraud Office* [1999] 2 AC 177 did not advert to this particular point, although Lord Hoffmann's observations, at p. 212E–G, indicated which way his sympathies would lie in connection with the use of disclosed material in open court, as in this case, before the Act of 1996, was passed. If the defendants wish to pursue this aspect of the case, which they cannot on the present interlocutory appeal, they would need a further ruling of the House of Lords on this specific point.

See also paras 12.94–12.95 of the Main Work.

This point was not the subject of a cross-appeal in *Campbell v Frisbee* [2003] **6.60** EMLR 76, [11].

(ii) Limitations

Further doubt has now been cast on the proposition that information about con- **6.62** victions cannot be protected as confidential by the decisions in *X and Y v News Group Newspapers and MGN Ltd* (see the Supplement to para 6.54 above) and the Court of Appeal in *R (Ellis) v Chief Constable of Essex Police* [2003] 2 FLR 566.

In *Ellis*, the Divisional Court was asked to rule on the lawfulness of an 'offender naming scheme' intended to be operated by the defendant as part of a crime prevention drive. The scheme was to have involved displaying posters at some forty public sites in the Brentwood area showing the name and the face of a selected offender, the nature of his offence and the sentence he was serving. The claimant, a serious offender with many convictions including for burglary and theft, was selected by the defendant to be the first offender featured in the scheme. A report of his latest conviction had been published in a local newspaper. Subsequently, because the defendant accepted that the claimant 'should . . . only be a candidate who is used for the purposes of the Scheme after a full reappraisal' (at [12]), the Court was requested to pronounce on the legality of the scheme in principle.

The Court (Lord Woolf CJ and Goldring J), applying *Hellewell v Chief Constable of Derbyshire* [1995] 1 WLR 804 and *R v Chief Constable of North Wales Police, ex p Thorpe* [1999] QB 396, decided that it was undesirable to rule on whether the scheme was in principle either lawful or unlawful; its legality would depend on the particular circumstances of each offender included in it and how the scheme was operated in practice. However, had it been required to rule on the claimant's individual case, it would have done so in his favour. The factors which told against the inclusion of the claimant in the scheme were: the defendant's superficial reaction to the risks for the claimant identified by the probation service; the risk of damage to the claimant's family and child who also had rights under Article 8; the possible unfairness of the scheme in discriminating between offenders who were included and those who were not; and the fact that those who were included would regard inclusion as a form of additional punishment. The second factor was seen as being of particular significance. The Court considered there was a real question whether it would ever be appropriate to include the father of a young child in the scheme.

The claim was made against a public authority, and the judgment of the Court did not dwell on the status of convictions *qua* confidential information. It was not in dispute that the claimant's Article 8 rights were engaged. Moreover, the Court, taking its lead from the Data Protection Act 1998, regarded a conviction as information personal or private to an offender: see [29]. On this basis, the only issue was whether the possible benefits of the scheme could be a necessary and proportionate justification for the interference with an individual offender's Article 8 rights. The Court expressed doubt that they ever could. Whether the same approach might be taken in a private law case brought in confidence against a media organisation must depend on the Court's attitude to the impact of Article 8 on private law causes of action. See the discussion of *Peck v UK*, in the Supplement to para 6.52 above.

Other information revealed in open court. For a fuller discussion of the im-   **6.63**
plied undertaking, the express duty imposed by CPR r 31.22 and parties' implied equitable duties of confidence in respect of documents and information
disclosed to them in the course of civil litigation, see paras 12.89–12.93 and
12.96–12.112 of the Main Work.

n180 In general, 'there can be nothing privileged or confidential in what passes
in open court': *Goldstone v Williams* [1899] 1 Ch 47, 52. This is of course subject to the duties imposed by the CPR. It was also held in *Goldstone v Williams,*
at 54, that depositions on the court file and open to public inspection are *pub-
lici iuris* and cannot be privileged from production. For a discussion of the status of information available on public registers, see the Supplement to paras
6.101–6.103 below. The lack of privilege or confidentiality in what passes in
open court is also subject to the Court's positive obligation to protect the Article
8 rights of individuals: see *Craxi (No 2) v Italy,* Application no 25337/94, judgment of 17 July 2003, and the Supplement to para 12.31 below.

(g) Financial and business information

(i) Scope

See also *Lady Archer v Williams* [2003] FSR 869, where Jackson J held at [49]   **6.64**
and [55] that all details of the claimant's financial affairs were protected by contractual and equitable duties of confidence owed by her personal assistant.

n185 See also *Cream Holdings Ltd v Banerjee* [2003] 3 WLR 999, [7], in which the
information in issue consisted of 'allegations of financial irregularities by Cream'.

n188 As regards the decision in *Fressoz and Roire v France* (2001) 31 EHRR 28
it is, nevertheless, to be noted that one ground of decision was that French domestic law (peculiarly) requires certain personal financial information to be
made publicly available: see [26], [48] and [53]. In relation to this point, see the
Supplement to para 6.102 below.

(h) Children's background, care, upbringing, and education

It does not follow from the fact that a parent owes a duty to the child that the par-   **6.65**
ent can sue in respect of third party disclosures of confidential information about
the child. For discussion of rights to protect the confidential information of others see paras 6.137–6.139 of the Main Work and cf Main Work para 6.36. In *Lady
Archer v Williams* a successful claim was made by a parent to restrain, in the law of
confidence, disclosure of information about sexual relationships engaged in by
her children: see [34]–[35]. The case is particularly striking given that the 'children' in question were all adults. However, this aspect of the claim was not ruled
on; it was not contested. As a matter of principle, it is only the person or persons

to whom confidence is owed that can assert the confidence. But that principle is subject to the further principle that there can be a shared right to assert a confidence: see the Supplement to para 6.137 below—and it may not always be worthwhile for a defendant to make a point on the non-joinder of parties, assuming they are able and willing to be joined.

(i) The contents of personal diaries, private correspondence, and conversations

(ii) Correspondence

6.68 See also *Philip v Pennell* [1907] 2 Ch 577, 586–7 *per* Kekewich J. By this time it was clearly an established general rule that, as a starting point, the contents of private letters were to be regarded as subject to a duty of confidentiality owed by the recipient to the writer. In *Lady Archer v Williams* Jackson J held that the contents of diaries kept by the claimant's personal assistant and details of certain conversations were protected by both contractual and equitable duties of confidence; it was conceded that the contents of correspondence were protected: see paras [34]–[35], [51] and [55]. But as regards conversations see para 6.69A of this Supplement below.

(iii) Private telephone conversations

6.69 There is of course no magic in the use of the telephone which confers confidentiality on a conversation. In *D v L* [2003] EWCA Civ 1169 the respondent made secret recordings of her conversations with the appellant to protect her in relation to domestic violence proceedings. The secretly recorded conversations did not involve the use of a phone. Injunctive relief was refused because, among other things, the information was in the public domain (see the Supplement to para 6.102 n336 below). However, Lord Phillips MR observed at [34] that 'on the face of it, publication of a covert tape recording of a private conversation involves a breach of confidence'.

The following paragraph has been inserted after paragraph 6.69:

(iv) Limitations

6.69A Some information about others contained in diaries, letters or conversations may not be capable of protection. In *Lady Archer v Williams* the claimant was denied protection in respect of the details of conversations between the defendant and the claimant's guests or visitors which did not relate to the claimant, her family, staff, or the defendant's duties as the claimant's personal assistant: see [50] and [82]. For reasons which are not clear, this approach was not carried through in the Court's ruling in respect of the diaries kept by the defendant; the entire content of these was protected. The refusal to protect information about third parties in *Lady Archer's* case may be contrasted with the approach of the PCC in its 1998 *Sir Elton*

John decision, which held that Sir Elton's privacy was infringed by the taking and publication of long lens photographs of the Beckhams relaxing as guests at his French home: Messrs Eversheds on behalf of Sir Elton John and *The Sport*, 2 July 1998 (Report 45).

(j) Home interior

In *Lady Archer v Williams* the confidentiality of the claimant's home security arrangements was conceded: see paras [34]–[35]. **6.70**

The cross-heading that precedes this paragraph in the Main Work should be replaced with a new sub-heading: '(k) **Collections of personal information**'. **6.71**

See the Supplement to para 3.109 above.

The cross-heading that precedes this paragraph in the Main Work should be replaced with a new sub-heading '(l) **Artistic and literary confidences**'. **6.72**

E. Criteria for Confidentiality

(2) Factors Indicating that Information is Confidential

(d) Created or imparted in confidential circumstances

n237 Lightman J's observations were not the subject of comment in the Court of Appeal in *Campbell v Frisbee*. Note also that in German law there is a right to privacy if the individual shuts himself off to some degree from the public at large and this exclusion was objectively obvious to third parties: *Caroline von Monaco II,* BGH NJW 1996, 1128–9 (translated by Raymond Youngs, copyright Professor Basil Markesinis, Institute of Global Law, Faculty of Laws, Bentham House, Endsleigh Gardens, London WC1H 0EG): **6.77**

> This can, for instance, be the case in separate rooms of a restaurant or in hotels, sports grounds, telephone booths, under certain circumstances even in the open, as long as the person does not appear more than just another member of the public . . . Moreover, the right to demand that other persons respect one's privacy presupposes that the situation in which the person [observed] finds himself is one of a typically private nature. This is the case where a person, relying on the seclusion of the specific place where he finds himself in, behaves in a manner which he would not normally adopt in full view of the public. This may be the case whenever [the observed person] expresses personal emotions which are clearly not intended for the eyes of third persons or is acting in an 'unrestrained' manner. Only in such situations can it be assumed and objectively verified that the person did not intend to allow other persons sharing the moment. In such circumstance he is entitled to have the chosen seclusion respected . . . It is an unjustified infringement of the sphere of privacy which is worthy of protection if, for reasons of personal gain, pictures are taken/published which exploit the innocence of the person depicted who believes

himself unobserved. This is always the case where the person is observed almost as if through a keyhole, or is surprised by the surreptitious taking of the pictures. The same applies where the picture is taken openly but so suddenly that the person photographed has no time to prepare himself. A restriction of the prohibition to these particular circumstances is justified because protection of the private sphere of life is here extended to places which are in theory open to everyone. In these cases the person's privacy is only unjustly infringed where the intrusion happened surreptitiously or by surprise.

This case is also referred to at para 3.81 of the Main Work and para 9.65 of this Supplement.

n238 See also *PG and JH v UK*, the relevant passage from which is set out at para 4.22 in the Main Work.

(g) Form or medium

6.80 **n248** Lindsay J at the trial of the *Douglas v Hello! Ltd* claim followed this approach (at [197]) and did not treat the information at issue differently because it had been recorded in digital form.

n251 In *D v L* (see the Supplement to para 6.69 above) the majority of the Court of Appeal noted that in *Douglas v Hello! Ltd* the point had been made that a photograph is distinct from the information it portrays, and held at [24] that:

> The same principle [is] applicable to a tape recording . . . of a private conversation . . . prima facie equity should impose a duty of confidence in relation to the tape quite separate and distinct from such obligation as may exist in relation to the information revealed on the tape

The reason given was that

> Just as a photograph can make a greater impact than an account of the matter depicted by that photograph, so the recorded details of the very words of a private conversation can make more impact, and cause more embarrassment and distress, than a mere account of the conversation in question.

However, it is important to focus on exactly what information is conveyed by a photograph; a street scene may not be confidential: see *Campbell v MGN Ltd* at [33], distinguishing *Douglas v Hello! Ltd* [2001] QB 967 on the facts. See further the Supplement to para 6.52 above.

(h) Qualities of the information

(ii) Not trivial, but useful or valuable

6.83 Although it is not entirely clear, the Court of Appeal in *Campbell v MGN Ltd* may have regarded the details of the claimant's attendance at Narcotics Anonymous as too trivial to warrant the protection of the law of confidence. The Court stated:

[53] . . . Given that it was legitimate for the defendants to publish the fact that Miss Campbell was a drug addict and that she was receiving treatment, it does not seem to us that it was particularly significant to add the fact that the treatment consisted of attendance at meetings of Narcotics Anonymous . . . [58] In summary, we differ from the judge in that we have concluded that the publication of information of which Miss Campbell complains was not, in its context, sufficiently significant to amount to a breach of duty owed to her.

See also *Douglas v Hello! Ltd* where Lindsay J held after the trial of the action, at [197], 'As I have said, the very fact that Hello! and OK! competed for exclusivity as they did and that each was ready to pay so much for it points to the commercial confidentiality of coverage of the event.'

n266 See too *Douglas v Hello! Ltd* at [195] and [197].

In *Lady Archer v Williams* at [67] Jackson J rejected an argument that the matters   **6.84**
there in issue fell into the category of 'trivial tittle tattle'. The matters in issue were wide-ranging and included '(e) details about the claimant's home life and any incident or conversation concerning any member of the claimant's family, guest, visitor or member of her staff which occurred in the claimant's home . . .': see [2003] FSR 869, [34]–[35].

(iii) Detailed and identifiable

The Court of Appeal's decision in *Campbell v MGN Ltd* demonstrates some of the   **6.85–6.86**
difficulties of attempting to draw a line between reporting a fact and reporting details about that fact, at least where there is a public interest in reporting the relevant fact. It was common ground in the case that publication of the fact that the claimant was undergoing therapy was legitimate. Morland J's finding that the disclosure of 'detail' of such therapy was nonetheless a breach of confidence was reversed by the Court of Appeal, which held at [62] that:

> such a story, without any background detail to support it, would have bordered on the absurd. We consider that the detail given, and indeed the photographs, were a legitimate if not an essential part of the journalistic package designed to demonstrate to the public that Miss Campbell had been deceiving the public when she said that she did not take drugs.

Applying *Fressoz and Roire v France*, the Court held at [64] that:

> provided that the publication of particular confidential information is justifiable in the public interest, the journalist must be given reasonable latitude as to the manner in which the information is conveyed to the public or his Article 10 right to freedom of expression will be unnecessarily inhibited.

It does not follow from this, however, that the publication of any detail will be justified on grounds of journalistic credibility: see *Ashdown v Telegraph Group Ltd* [2002] Ch 149.

(3) Inaccessibility: the Public Domain

(a) Information in the public domain is not confidential

6.89   The decision of Lindsay J in *Douglas v Hello! Ltd* suggests that photographs, considered as conveying confidential information, may be differently treated from information conveyed verbally or in other ways, so far as concerns inaccessibility or the public domain: [196], [209], [213], [217]–[221], [278]. In this regard, see also paras 6.80–6.81 of the Main Work and the Supplement to the notes thereto above. The unauthorised pictures of the Douglas' wedding, which were the subject of the complaint, were in the event published by the *Hello!* defendants simultaneously with publication of the authorised pictures by or with the consent of the claimants: [204]. This came about because the *Hello!* defendants' planned earlier publication was held up by the interim injunction, which the Court of Appeal discharged. The confidential information, which was the subject of protection, was what the couple (and no doubt the event) looked like on the exceptional occasion of their wedding: [197]. It was argued for the *Hello!* defendants that this previously confidential information ceased to have the necessary attribute of inaccessibility and passed into the public domain, with publication of extensive images in *OK!*. Lindsay J rejected this argument, on the ground that a claimant, who was denied an injunction at the interim stage on the ground that he *intended* to make the information public, and therefore that damages were an adequate remedy, could not at trial be met by the argument that damages were precluded, because he had carried into effect his intention to publish. That, said the judge, would negate the finding at the interim stage that damages were an adequate remedy: [213].

Nor was the grant of a perpetual injunction after the trial precluded by information having passed into the public domain. The judge held that 'given that the far better authorised pictures were also . . . put into the public domain . . . the look of the unauthorised photographs has passed out of the public mind': [278].

Earlier decisions on applications for interim injunctions in cases concerning unauthorised photography of confidential subject matter suggest that release of the subject matter into the public domain by publication of authorised photographs or film may preclude any remedy in respect of publication of unauthorised images thereafter. See *Shelley Films Ltd v Rex Features Ltd* [1994] EMLR 134, 151 where the deputy judge recognised that release of the confidential information to the public by the claimant would result in the loss of the right to protection. In *Creation Records Ltd v News Group Newspapers Ltd* [1997] EMLR 444, the question did not arise, since it was clear that the threatened publication of an unauthorised picture by the *Sun* newspaper long ante-dated the planned release to the public of the authorised image.

(b) Public domain is a question of fact and degree

There is a tension between the approach taken by the Court to the 'inaccessibility' **6.90** criterion in two recent first instance decisions in commercial confidentiality cases. In *Douglas v Hello! Ltd,* Lindsay J took the view that if the information at issue was inaccessible, that alone was sufficient to satisfy the first limb of the *Coco v Clark* test, although other factors were relevant when considering whether to grant relief. See the Supplement to para 6.11 n32 above. By contrast, in *Cray Valley v Deltech Europe Ltd* [2003] EWHC 728 (Ch) Jacob J found that inaccessibility was a necessary but not a sufficient condition for a claim in confidence; that something more was required. He stated at [52] that:

> there is a low threshold to be crossed before information passes from the unprotected public property and public knowledge to the protectable trade secret, that inaccessibility by the public is a particular touchstone . . .

and seemed to accept that the claimants had surmounted that threshold. However, he went on to find that 'even so, I do not think the information here is properly to be regarded as confidential'. In dismissing the confidence claim, at [54]–[55], Jacob J held that:

> so much was published, so much was second nature to the team, so much of the recipes were not critical and were easy to reverse engineer, that a man of conscience would not say 'here is a specific trade secret which I may not use' . . . the point is that unless information is obviously confidential (e.g. because it is obviously likely to be of significant value to a competitor) the law does not step in where the 'owner' of the alleged trade secret himself does not bother to protect it.

In the sphere of personal information, see also *Peck v UK* at [62]:

> As a result, the relevant moment was viewed to an extent which far exceeded any exposure to a passer-by or to security observation . . . and to a degree surpassing that which the applicant could possibly have foreseen when he walked in Brentwood on 20 August 1995.

This passage suggests that a person may have an Article 8 right to object to widespread dissemination of even relatively accessible information, the yardstick being the claimant's reasonable expectations as to the degree of publicity that would ensue in the circumstances of what he was doing.

What constitutes disclosure, or publication, of confidential information, and who is responsible in law where there is a publication, are two questions related to this. For some purposes there would be good reason to assimilate disclosure of confidential information to publication of a libel, since the same communication may very well amount to both (see paras 7.47–7.50 of the Main Work). On the other hand the libel definition creates a very low threshold for liability, which will be inappropriate in some cases. In libel a limited disclosure is often subject to a defence of qualified privilege, but it may be thought that in some cases of disclosure of confidential information, there should be no risk of liability at all, or, in other words, complete immunity from suit. On what constitutes publication in other contexts, see also *Re M (A Child)(Children and Family Reporter: Disclosure)* [2003] Fam 26 [21], [65]–[67], and on the question of responsibility for publication (ie who counts as a wrongdoer, when publication has in fact occurred), see *Douglas v Hello! Ltd* [2003] EMLR 585 [33] (on appeal from Laddie J), and see the Supplement to paras 4.44 and 5.15 above.

(e) Cases where general disclosure is imminent

6.97 In *Douglas v Hello! Ltd* at [186(viii)] Lindsay J found that the fact that 'authorised publication is due in a moment . . . may make it harder for the unauthorised publisher to justify his breach'. He explained at [224] why he did not regard *Times Newspapers Ltd v Mirror Group Newspapers Ltd* [1993] EMLR 443 as authoritative in the post Human Rights Act age. *Exchange Telegraph v Gregory* [1896] 1 QB 147 concerned unpublished information about stock prices bought from the London Stock Exchange. The information was held to be confidential where authorised publication was due in a moment.

(f) Confidentiality in personal information may survive publicity

6.99 n327 See *A v M (Family Proceedings: Publicity)* [2000] 1 FLR 562, a case consistent with the approach stated in para 6.98 of the Main Work, in which Charles J granted an injunction against a mother and her partner from republishing to the media information about the wishes, behaviour, and conduct of her children, notwithstanding that much of it had already been placed in the public domain, on the grounds that further publication of such information could be damaging to the children.

More recently, in *Re S (Publicity)* [2003] HRLR 911, Hedley J modified a *contra mundum* injunction to permit the name and identity of the defendant and victim in a murder trial to be reported during the trial, even though it would lead to the identification of the seven-year-old brother of the deceased. This decision was upheld on appeal on grounds which included the fact that the information was already well known within the area in which the child lived, so that the order would have only a mitigating effect. The judge, nevertheless, refused to qualify the injunction with a public domain proviso. At [20], Hedley J held, 'in my judgment, on the issue of re-publication of past information, the balance clearly falls the other way and there can be no real detriment to any public interest. In so refusing, I am following the path already illuminated by Charles J in his judgment in *A v M (Family Proceedings: Publicity)*.' There was no appeal against this decision.

For a commercial case where confidentiality was held to survive substantial publication see *Exchange Telegraph v Central News* [1897] 2 Ch 48 (information about the results of race meetings in Manchester which was known to those who attended).

See also the Supplement to para 6.89 above.

(4) Other Factors Negating Confidentiality

The last two sentences of this para in the Main Work should read as follows: 'Cases **6.100** in which a claim for breach of confidence may be met by the justifications or defences of public interest or "just cause or excuse", of which, what follows may be described as particular aspects, are addressed further in Chapter 9 below.'

Additional authorities which may be cited in support of the existence of a public **6.102** policy rule excluding from the ambit of confidentiality information which is required to be disclosed to the public include *Goldstone v Williams* (see the Supplement to para 6.63 n180 above), where information on publicly accessible court records was held to fall outside the scope of any claim to litigation privilege, and *Initial Services v Putterill* [1968] 1 QB 396, where the Court of Appeal held it arguable that information was not confidential in nature because, although not in fact a matter of public knowledge, it was required by law to be placed on a public register. See in particular *per* Lord Denning MR at 406. To somewhat similar effect are the observations of Lindsay J in *Douglas v Hello! Ltd*, commenting on the *Lenah Game Meats* case at [190], where he observed that 'the fact that the operations were and had to be licensed by a public authority suggested that information about the nature of the operations was not confidential'. Also, it can be observed, as noted in the Supplement to para 6.64 above, that one of the key reasons why the ECtHR found in *Fressoz and Roire v France* that there had been a violation of the applicants' rights under Article 10 was that to some extent the information they had been fined for publishing was information that French law required to be made available to the public: see (2001) 31 EHRR 28, [26], [48] and [53].

n336 In *D v L* [2003] EWCA Civ 1169 the Court of Appeal appears to have taken the same approach as was adopted in *Elliott* and *Bunn*, treating the information in question as being in the public domain 'having been revealed in evidence and made the subject of a finding in the . . . judgment': see [19] *per* Waller LJ and, to similar effect, [34](iii) *per* Lord Phillips MR.

As noted in para 4.21 of the Main Work, the Calcutt Committee on Privacy (at para 12.17 of its Report) saw merit in specifically excluding from the ambit of personal information to be protected by a privacy law 'any material . . . required by law to be registered, recorded or otherwise available to public inspection'. Such a rule would be consistent with the position in the United States, where the law precludes an action for invasion of privacy in respect of accurate disclosure of information contained in public records, regardless of the extent of actual knowledge:

see Restatement of Torts (2d) §652D, the United States Supreme Court decisions in *Cox Broadcasting Corp v Cohen* 420 US 469, 494–5 and *Landmark Communications Inc v Virginia* 435 US 829, 840, and the decision of the Supreme Court of Iowa in *Howard v Des Moines Register and Tribune Company* (1979) 283 NW 2d 289, 298-290. See also R D Sack, *Sack on Defamation* (1999), at para 12.4.5.5, in which this US law principle is analysed.

However, it could be argued that such an approach is hard to reconcile with two recently decided cases on the naming of criminals, *X and Y v News Group Newspapers and MGN Ltd* [2003] FSR 850 and *R (Ellis) v Chief Constable of Essex Police* [2003] 2 FLR 566, (see the Supplement to paras 2.14, 6.54 and 6.62 above) and the scheme of the Data Protection Act 1998, at least in respect of information about crime. Information 'as to the commission or alleged commission by [an individual] of any offence' and 'any proceedings for any offence committed or alleged to have been committed by [the individual], the disposal of such proceedings or the sentence of any court in such proceedings', which obviously includes criminal convictions, are defined in s 2 of the 1998 Act as sensitive personal data. Such data cannot be processed lawfully by a data controller except where both a Schedule 2 and a Schedule 3 condition can be met: see paras 5.31ff of the Main Work. The fact that such data form part of a public record or are information required by law to be made available to the public is not of itself sufficient to satisfy such conditions. Moreover, the media exemption under s 32 of the Act applies only if, among other things, the media organ reasonably believes that publication would be in the public interest, and this may be said to imply that an evaluative exercise must be carried out in each individual case.

(b) Other information about crime and iniquity

6.103 See also the observations made in *Campbell v Frisbee* [2002] EWHC 328 (Ch), [7] referred to in para 6.60 in the Main Work and in the Supplement thereto.

F. The Duty of Confidence

(1) When Will Duties of Confidence be Imposed?

(a) Express Contract

(i) Principles

6.105 n344 See now also the judgment of the Court of Appeal in *Campbell v Frisbee* and in *Cream Holdings Ltd v Banerjee* (in which, at [65], Simon Brown LJ observed that the judge had granted an interim injunction 'above all because of Ms Banerjee's "undoubted obligations of confidentiality" which, he accepted, having regard to her employment as an in-house chartered accountant placed her under a "high-level duty"') and the Supplement to para 6.109 below. See also the decision of Jackson J that the employee's contractual obligation of confidentiality survives the termination of the contract in *Lady Archer v Williams* [2003] FSR 869 [48].

See *R v Her Majesty's Attorney-General for England and Wales* [2003] EMLR 24 **6.106** where, following damaging disclosures by serving members of the SAS, the Ministry of Defence considered that it was necessary to restrict by contract publication of any information by serving members 'relating to the work of, or in support of, the United Kingdom Special Forces' without prior authorisation.

The proposition in the last sentence of this paragraph of the Main Work has been **6.108** cast into doubt by the Court of Appeal's decision in *Campbell v Frisbee*. The Court held that the question of what effect repudiation has on a contractual duty of confidence was not suitable for summary determination under CPR r 24. The Court 'did not believe that the effect of the duties of confidence assumed under contract when the contract in question is wrongfully repudiated is clearly established': see [34]. A separate issue is the extent to which an equitable duty of confidence will survive a termination of contractual relations. It does not appear to have been in dispute in *Campbell v Frisbee* that the equitable duty survives.

(ii) Limitations

Again, the proposition in the second sentence of this paragraph of the Main Work **6.109** has been called into question by the Court of Appeal in *Campbell v Frisbee*. At [22], the Court held it arguable that 'a duty of confidentiality that has been expressly assumed under contract carries more weight, when balanced against the restriction of the right of freedom of expression, than a duty of confidentiality that is not buttressed by express agreement'. In this regard, there appears to be a tension between the view of the Court of Appeal in this case and that expressed by it in *London Regional Transport Ltd v The Mayor of London* [2003] EMLR 88, [46].

(b) The equitable obligation of confidence

(iii) Cases where there is a relationship giving rise to a duty of confidence

The reference to *A v B plc* in this para of the Main Work should be to *A v B and C*. **6.116**

Non-contractual relationships generally. In *D v L* (see the Supplement to para **6.118** 6.69 above) the critical factors imposing a duty of confidence on L were held to be that the tape recordings she had made of conversations with her live-in partner, D 'were being taken secretly, related to private matters being discussed in a private conversation and were taped without the consent of D': see [26] *per* Waller LJ.

n379 See the Supplement to para 6.108 above. **6.119**

(iv) Cases where there is no pre-existing relationship

6.125   In *Istil Group Inc v Zahoor* [2003] 2 All ER 252, the Court analysed the rationale of the principles expounded in *Ashburton v Pape*. The case was concerned with whether a remedy was available to restrain the use of privileged communications between a party to litigation and a witness, or potential witness, when the latter chooses to disclose them to an opposing party. Lawrence Collins J considered the long line of authorities from *Ashburton v Pape*, concluding at [74] as follows:

> First, it is clear that the jurisdiction to restrain the use of privileged documents is based on the equitable jurisdiction to restrain breach of confidence. The citation of the cases on the duty of confidentiality of an employee makes it plain that what the Court of Appeal was doing in *Lord Ashburton v Pape* was applying the law of confidentiality in order to prevent disclosure of documents which would otherwise have been privileged, and were and remained confidential. Second, after a privileged document has been seen by the opposing party, the court may intervene by way of injunction in exercise of the equitable jurisdiction if the circumstances warrant such intervention on equitable grounds. Third, if the party in whose hands the document has come (or his solicitor) either (a) has procured inspection of the document by fraud or (b) on inspection, realises that he has been permitted to see the document only by reason of an obvious mistake, the court has the power to intervene by the grant of an injunction in exercise of the equitable jurisdiction. Fourth, in such cases the court should ordinarily intervene, unless the case is one where the injunction can properly be refused on the general principles affecting the grant of a discretionary remedy, e.g. on the ground of delay.

The Court held at [112], that:

> this is a case in which, in the exercise of the *Lord Ashburton v Pape* jurisdiction, the court is entitled to balance the public interest in supporting legal professional privilege on the one hand, and the public interest in the proper administration of justice on the other hand . . . In my judgment the combination of forgery and misleading evidence make this a case where the equitable jurisdiction to restrain breach of confidence gives way to the public interest in the proper administration of justice.

(c) Equitable duties on the media and other third party recipients

(i) Acquisition from the person owing the duty

6.132–6.133   Morland J's rejection of the 'dishonesty requirement' was upheld by the Court of Appeal in *Campbell v MGN Ltd*. The Court held at [69] that:

> dishonesty is not an appropriate word to use in relation to the publication of information about someone's private life in circumstances which would make the publication offensive to any fair-minded person. We consider that the media can fairly be expected to identify confidential information about an individual's private life which, absent good reason, it will be offensive to publish.

(e) The position of those on notice of injunctions against others

As to the position of third parties on notice of final as opposed to interim **6.136** injunctions in confidence, see now *Jockey Club v Buffham* [2003] QB 462, where Gray J held that third parties are not affected by such orders and will not be in contempt of court if they destroy the confidentiality which the final injunction seeks to protect. The Court's reasoning in *Jockey Club v Buffham* was based to some extent on *obiter* observations of the Court of Appeal in *A-G v Punch Ltd* [2001] QB 1028. While the Attorney-General appealed successfully from the Court of Appeal's decision in the latter case to the House of Lords ([2003] 2 WLR 49), their Lordships did not address the issue raised or the principle stated by Gray J in the *Jockey Club* case.

In an appropriate case, to avoid the risk of the confidentiality of his information being destroyed by third parties, a successful claimant at the conclusion of the proceedings might seek to rely on *Venables v News Group Newspapers Ltd* and *X and Y v News Group Newspapers* (see the Supplement to para 6.54 above) to obtain an injunction *contra mundum*. A possible alternative, namely interim relief against unnamed defendants identified by description and/or by reference to the acts they may perform, is indicated by the decisions of Laddie J in *Bloomsbury Publishing Group Ltd v News Group Newspapers Ltd and others* [2003] EWHC 1807 (Ch) and of Morritt V-C in the same case: [2003] 1 WLR 1633.

(2) *Who Can Sue for Breach of Confidence?*

(a) Who has the right of confidence?

In *Douglas v Hello! Ltd* Lindsay J applied *Gilbert v The Star Newspaper Co Ltd* **6.137** (1894) 11 TLR 3 and *O Mustad & Son v Dosen and another* [1964] 1 WLR 109 so as to conclude that a right of confidence may be the subject of co-ownership 'at any rate where the defendant knew or could be taken to have known of the co-ownership or sharing before acting in breach and where all entitled to the confidence assert it': [187].

n437 The first reference in this note should be to *Nationwide Building Society v* **6.139** *Various Solicitors (No 2)* (HC, 30 March 1998, Blackburne J).

In *R (Ellis) v Chief Constable of Essex Police*, the privacy rights of the claimant's family, especially his young child, were the most significant factor in the Court's considerations, albeit that they were not parties to the proceedings. See the Supplement to para 6.62 above.

n439 The decision of the Court of Appeal in *Ashworth Hospital Authority v MGN Ltd* was affirmed by the House of Lords: [2002] 1 WLR 2033.

(b) Assignment of rights of action

6.140 n441 See too *Douglas v Hello! Ltd* at [187] (where Lindsay J speaks of sharing the benefit of the obligation) and the Supplement to para 6.137. The word 'assignment' in this paragraph is derived from *Murray v Yorkshire Fund Managers Ltd* [1998] 1 WLR 951 at 959b, and should be substituted by the word 'sharing', which is also used in *Ashworth Hospital Authority v MGN Ltd* [2001] 1 WLR 515, para 52.

(3) Misuse: the Nature, Scope, and Duration of the Duty

(a) Scope of the duty

(ii) The equitable duty

6.144 See also *D v L* (Supplement to para 6.69 above) at [26]:

> . . . equity should . . . impose on the conscience of the person who secretly takes tapes of a private conversation relating to private matters for a purpose that may be justified an obligation not to use the same for any other purpose.

As noted in para 6.46 of the Main Work, it is not a breach of confidence or privacy to disclose or use personal medical information for a purpose other than that for which it was confided or obtained, if the individual to whom it relates is not identifiable: see *R v Dept of Health, ex p Source Informatics Ltd* [2001] QB 424, *H (A Healthcare Worker) v Associated Newspapers Ltd* [2002] EMLR 425 and *X v Y* [1988] 2 All ER 648, all of which were argued on this footing. The same may apply to the use and disclosure of other kinds of personal information. The disclosure or other processing of personal data in circumstances where the individual to whom it relates is not identifiable falls outside the scope of the Data Protection legislation: see paras 4.42 and 5.20 of the Main Work. The European Court's approach appears to be that if the identity of the individual to whom the private information relates has been effectively concealed, then that individual's Article 8 rights are not even engaged. Moreover, it seems that an imperfect attempt at concealment will have a significant bearing on whether the alleged interference with Article 8 is proportionate and justified: see *Peck v UK* at [61], [62] and [80]–[85] and *Friedl v Austria* (1996) 21 EHRR 83.

Not everyone, however, thinks that anonymisation is enough to avoid a successful claim for breach of *privacy.* The pertinent facts, issues, and result of the New Zealand case *L v G* [2002] DCR 34 were as follows. The plaintiff was in a sexual relationship with the defendant during the course of which a number of sexually explicit photographs of the plaintiff were taken, one of which was published in an adult magazine by the defendant. The plaintiff consented to the taking of the photos; she did not consent to their publication in the magazine. L conceded that, apart from a distinctive garment she was wearing that some who knew her might recognise, and part of which was visible, she would not be identified from the photograph. One of the issues the judge therefore discussed was whether the public disclosure of private facts must result in the identification of the person to whom the facts relate. The judge identified privacy as a value which was peculiarly personal in the sense that it reinforced a psychological need of the person to preserve an intrusion-free zone of personality and family, with the result that there was always anguish when that zone was violated. If this was so, then the rights protected by the tort related to the loss of the personal shield of privacy, rather than issues of perception and identification. He found that the fact that L could not be identified did not prevent her from recovering for any breach of her privacy, but could be reflected in any assessment of damages.

Could this approach be followed in England? If the view expressed by Lord Mustill in the *Dixons* case [2001] QB 885 [48] that 'an infringement of privacy is an affront to the personality, which is damaged both by the violation and by the demonstration that personal space is not inviolate' were to prevail more generally, it might well be.

(iii) Duration of the duty of confidence

In relation to the proposition stated in the first sentence of this paragraph see *Gunn-Russo v Nugent Care Society* [2002] 1 FLR 1.   **6.145**

n451 See now the judgment of the Court of Appeal in *Campbell v Frisbee*.

n454 See also the discussion in the Supplement to para 6.99 above.

n455 For a further discussion of *R v BCC, ex p Granada Television Ltd* [1995] EMLR 163, including an outline of the facts of the case, see para 13.45 of the Main Work.

See *Craxi (No 2) v Italy*, Application no 25337/94, judgment of 17 July 2003 and the Supplement to para 4.55 above.   **6.146**

n456 See also para 4.55 of the Main Work. In *Wilson v Wyatt* (1820) referred to in para 6.43 of the Main Work, in contrast with the modern guidance issued to physicians, Lord Eldon appears to have assumed that the doctor's duty of medical confidentiality ended or ceased to be enforceable on the death of the patient.

The PCC, in an adjudication of May 2003, rejected a privacy complaint made on behalf of Father John Tolkien, deceased, in respect of a sensational newspaper article published between his death and his funeral which accused him of abusing dozens of young boys in a career of depravity. The PCC explained this decision as follows: 'The Commission did not consider that questions of privacy and intrusion could relate to the deceased or that, as publication had been subsequent to the death of Father Tolkien, it could consider this aspect of the complaint further:' Messrs Manches on behalf of the Tolkein family and *Sunday Mercury* (Report 62).

(b) Is detriment to the claimant necessary?

6.148   The 'offensiveness' test (see the Supplement to paras 6.12 and 6.42 above) can be viewed as a threshold requirement for liability which fulfils the same function as the disputed detriment requirement.

G. The Role of Confidence in Media Privacy Cases

(1) The Use of Confidence Claims to Protect Privacy

(c) The 'label' of privacy

6.151   In *Campbell v MGN Ltd* the Court of Appeal was not asked to consider the creation of a new tort of privacy (by which was meant intrusion into privacy which did not involve the disclosure of private facts, discussed in paras 3.13–3.21 of the Main Work) but to apply the law of confidence: see [30]–[35]. However, it held that the unjustifiable publication of information relating to 'an aspect of an individual's private life which he does not choose to make public . . . would be better described as a breach of privacy rather than a breach of confidence': see [69], [70]. These passages, and *A v B plc*, indicate a growing recognition by the Court that privacy is now more than a 'label' and that the principles developed in relation to the law of confidence in a commercial context are not automatically transferable to the context of personal confidential information. The cause of action of privacy appears to be turning into a different creature from confidence. Nevertheless, in *Douglas v Hello! Ltd*, Lindsay J at [229] declined the invitation to hold that there was 'an existing law of privacy under which the 1st and 2nd claimants are entitled to relief'.

The House of Lords has now ruled that English law does not recognise a general tort of invasion of privacy: *Wainwright v Home Office* [2003] 3 WLR 1137 [35]. However, referring to the remarks of Sedley LJ in *Douglas v Hello! Ltd* cited in this paragraph of the Main Work Lord Hoffmann commented at [30]: 'His observations are in my opinion no more (although certainly no less) than a plea for the extension and possibly renaming of the old action for breach of confidence. As Buxton LJ pointed out in this case in the Court of Appeal . . . such an extension would go further than any English court has yet gone and would be contrary to some cases (such as *Kaye v Robertson* [1991] FSR 62) in which it positively declined to do so. The question must wait for another day.'

(2) Identifying the Privacy Interests at Stake

(a) The importance of identifying the interests

6.152   n477 This does not mean that Article 10 rights are to be given priority over Article

8 rights: see *Douglas v Hello! Ltd* [2001] QB 967, at [135] *per* Sedley LJ, and [2003] 3 All ER 996, at 186(v) *per* Lindsay J. See also the Supplement to para 9.53 below and G Phillipson, 'Transforming Breach of Confidence? Towards a Common Law Right of Privacy under the Human Rights Act' [2003] 66:5 MLR 726, 748–58.

(b) Progress in analysing the concept of privacy

n486 See para 6.98 in the Main Work.   **6.154**

(c) The distinction between privacy and commercial interests

In *Douglas v Hello! Ltd* Lindsay J analysed the claimants' rights as being in the na-   **6.155**
ture of a trade secret and as such capable of being protected on conventional lines:
[195]–[196].

n489 This appears to reflect the distinction drawn in the United States and other legal systems between the private facts tort and publicity rights. In this regard, see Chapter 3 of the Main Work generally and the Supplement to para 6.37 above.

(d) Future developments

n492 It can be observed that in *Campbell v MGN Ltd* at [59]–[61] the Court of   **6.156**
Appeal did not view 'with enthusiasm' the attempt by the defendant to draw an
analogy between the reliance on public interest to justify publication of confidential material and the defence of qualified privilege to a claim for defamation with
reference to principles derived from the privacy laws of the United States and
South Africa.

(3) Privacy and Confidentiality Compared

Campbell v MGN Ltd furnishes another example of conduct which may consti-   **6.157**
tute a breach of privacy but not a breach of confidence. The defendant published
photographs of the claimant in the street, taken without her consent. As noted in
the Supplement to para 6.52 above, the Court of Appeal held that the publication
was not a breach of confidence. It considered that this aspect of the case 'exempli-
fied the distinction' between breach of confidence and breach of privacy: 'without
the caption the photographs were invasive but did not convey confidential information'. The claimant had expressly abstained from pursuing a case that English
law should recognise a right of privacy which would make such publication a tort:
see [31]–[34] and the Supplement to para 6.52 above. At [54] the Court appeared
to leave open the question of whether a person would have a cause of action for
breach of privacy alone in such circumstances on the basis that 'the reader might
have found it offensive that what were obviously covert photographs had been
taken of her' (as discussed in paras 2.28–2.29 and 2.34 of the Main Work). It was

noted, however, that in the case itself it was conceded that 'that, of itself, is not re-lied upon as a ground for legal complaint'. The decision of the ECtHR in *Peck v UK* further illustrates the difference between confidentiality and privacy (see the Supplement to paras 6.40 n110 and 6.52 above).

n497 Now, see also *Campbell v MGN Ltd* and *Peck v UK*. The claimant in *Campbell v MGN Ltd* has successfully petitioned the Appeal Committee of the House of Lords for leave to appeal from the decision of the Court of Appeal. The appeal is due to be heard in February 2004.

7

PRIVACY AND DEFAMATION

A. Introduction

(2) Essential Features of Defamation

Publication in the law of defamation does not have the ordinary meaning of giv- **7.03**
ing publicity, but means any communication by one person to another (other
than the subject of the communication). The law of defamation also has all embracing rules as to who is a joint tortfeasor where publication in fact occurs: see
Gatley on Libel and Slander (10th edn, 2004) para 6.15, 6.18. Such a low threshold for liability for contempt of court was rejected by the Court of Appeal in interpreting 'publication' in the Administration of Justice Act 1960, s 12, in *Re M
(A Child)(Children and Family Reporter: Disclosure)* [2003] Fam 26 [21],
[65]–[67]. On the other hand, since the same communication may be both a disclosure of private facts, and defamatory, there are arguments for adopting the

same definition of publication, whether the claim be in defamation, confidentiality or privacy (cf paras 7.47–7.50 of the Main Work). On the question of responsibility for publication (ie who counts as a wrongdoer, when publication has in fact occurred), see *Douglas v Hello! Ltd* [2003] EMLR 585 [33] (on appeal from Laddie J) and the Supplement to paras 4.48, 5.15, and 6.90 above.

B. Protection of Privacy by Defamation Law

(1) Right Thinking Members of Society

7.11　n9 *Jackson v MGN Ltd* (CA, 17 March 1994) referred to in the Main Work is reported in The Times, 29 March 1994. Contrary to what is stated in the Main Work, Jackson in fact underwent a medical examination prior to the case settling shortly before trial.

(3) Fair Comment on a Matter of Public Interest

7.15　n18 *Branson v Bower* is now reported at [2002] 2 QB 737.

C. Conflict Between Defamation and Privacy

(1) The Controversy over Truth as an Absolute Defence

(d) Article 8 of the European Convention on Human Rights

7.27　In *Cumpana and Mazare v Romania*, Application no 33348/96, judgment of 10 June 2003, the ECtHR unanimously held that reputation and honour are equally protected by Articles 8 and 10(2) of the Convention: [48] and the Dissenting Opinion, last paragraph. The case related to an allegation of a corrupt relationship between two lawyers while they had held posts in a local authority. One of the lawyers was a man, the other a woman who had become a judge. The article was illustrated with a cartoon showing the couple arm in arm carrying a bag of money, and addressing each other in terms of familiarity. The woman is depicted saying 'if you become an advocate, I will become a judge, and we will have enough to go round the world'. Part of the complaint by them in the national courts was that this suggested they were having an extra-marital affair, each of them being married to others. This allegation was untrue, and the Court held that it was an interference with their right to respect for their private and family life: [12]–[13], [56].

(e) The conflict between obligations of disclosure and the right to privacy

7.29　n41 In the Main Work the reference to *Gaskin v UK*, Series A No 160 should be (1990) 12 EHRR 36.

n43 *Bennett v Compass Group UK and Ireland Ltd* is now reported at [2002] ICR   **7.30**
1177.

(3) The Conflict Between the Rule Against Prior Restraint and the Right to Privacy

(a) The rule against prior restraint

In *Cream Holdings Ltd v Banerjee* [2003] 2 All ER 318 the Court of Appeal held   **7.35**
that on a true construction of s 12(3) of the Human Rights Act 1998 the threshold test to be applied when considering whether or not to grant an injunction to
restrain publication before trial is that of a real prospect of success, convincingly
established [12], [56], [83], [93]. The claimants were a group of companies with
a range of business interests; the defendants were its former accountant (Ms
Banerjee) and the publisher of the *Liverpool Echo*. Ms Banerjee made allegations
to the newspaper of financial irregularities by the claimants. The claimants sought
an injunction until trial to restrain publication in breach of confidence to which
the defendants raised a defence of 'public interest'.

Section 12(3) HRA provides:

> No . . . relief is to be granted so as to restrain publication before trial unless the court
> is satisfied that the applicant is *likely to establish* that publication should not be al-
> lowed (emphasis added).

The meaning of 'likely to establish' was crucial to the decision whether or not to
grant the injunction. Both Simon Brown and Sedley LJJ considered that the more
obvious meaning of the words was 'more likely than not to establish' rather than
'has a real prospect of establishing' [58], [69], [71] but that to adopt this construction would be necessarily to rank the right to freedom of expression above all
possible countervailing rights, including other Convention rights [51]–[52],
[59], [77]–[83]. This would be contrary to s 3 of the Human Rights Act which requires that all legislation (including therefore s 12(3)) 'be read and given effect in
a way which is compatible with the Convention rights'. Therefore, in any contest
between Convention rights no presumptive priority is given to freedom of expression.

The position is different in regard to the qualifying matters referred to in Article
10(2), where these are not convention rights but, in the language of Sedley LJ [81]
'convention values'. In a conflict between 'convention values' and freedom of expression in Article 10, freedom of expression will enjoy presumptive priority
[54]–[55], [81] and any interference must be strictly justified. Accordingly different principles apply in interim injunctions to restrain publication according to
whether or not the claimant relies on a Convention right.

On this reasoning it is crucial to know whether protection of reputation is a
Convention right, or not. In *Cumpana and Mazare v Romania*, Application no

33348/96, judgment of 10 June 2003, the ECtHR unanimously held that reputation and honour are equally protected by Article 8 and Article 10(2) of the Convention. That was a case where the allegation complained of was of an extra-marital affair, which was held to be an interference with the private and family life of the complainants in the national courts. There were also allegations of financial impropriety against the same individuals. It was because the majority held that the allegations of the extra-marital affair went beyond the bounds of acceptable criticism, that the Court held that the interference with the freedom of expression of the applicant publishers was proportionate, and that there was therefore no breach of Article 10: [57] and [60]. It is for consideration whether the same conclusion would have followed had the Court held that only the financial allegations went beyond the bounds of acceptable criticism. It appears that the result would have been the same, that is to say that the Court was not making a distinction of principle between reputation in relation to sexual matters and reputation in relation to financial matters. The fact that the allegation of sexual impropriety was not alleged to be true was obviously material to the majority's decision that the allegation exceeded the bounds of acceptable criticism. The minority considered that satire should not be discouraged, and would have held that the interference with the applicant publishers' Article 10 rights was disproportionate.

Although the Court of Appeal in *Cream Holdings v Banerjee* did not directly address the question whether s 12(3) altered the law as regards interim injunctions in defamation, the assumption seems to have been that it did not: [43], [96]. Besides, s 12(3) provides merely the threshold test. As was pointed out by Simon Brown LJ at [61] it does not follow that an interim injunction will be granted whenever 'the lower threshold test' of reasonable prospect of success is satisfied. 'On the contrary, the lower threshold test merely gives the court a discretion in a greater number of cases. Often the court will not think it right to exercise that discretion in favour of prior restraint unless it is indeed satisfied that the claim will more probably than not succeed at trial.'

However, it is suggested that in any case where the claimant seeks to restrain publication before trial, the Court must first consider whether or not the claim involves a Convention right. In cases where the publication sought to be restrained is of information of a personal nature, whether or not also defamatory, the Court must consider whether publication would infringe the claimant's Article 8 rights. If so, the Court must look at both whether the claimant can justify an interference with the defendant's Article 10 right and whether the defendant can justify an interference with the claimant's Article 8 right. See H Tomlinson QC and Heather Rogers, 'Privacy Injunctions: Reviewing the Approach' in New Law Journal, 30 May 2003.

If the claim does not involve a Convention right then in defamation cases against defendants who raise the defence of justification the long-standing rule in *Bonnard v Perryman* [1892] 2 Ch 269 will no doubt continue to be applied.

In *Cream Holdings v Banerjee* the Court of Appeal did not agree with the Vice-Chancellor in *Imutran Ltd v Uncaged Campaigns Ltd* [2001] 2 All ER 385 at [17] that the difference was only slight as between the tests under s 12(3) and *American Cyanamid*. The Court of Appeal highlighted an important distinction between the threshold test created by s 12(3) of a real prospect of success convincingly established and the *American Cyanamid* requirement to show merely a good arguable case. By contrast with *American Cyanamid*, when applying the test under s 12(3) the Court is required to consider the merits of the claim for injunctive relief so as to reach a judgment as to the prospects of eventual success, and cannot grant relief unless satisfied on cogent evidence that the claim does indeed have a real prospect of success at trial: [56], [121]–[123].   **7.36**

n63 *A v B plc* is now reported at [2003] QB 195, CA.

(b) Priority given to the rule against prior restraint

In *Cream Holdings v Banerjee* the Court of Appeal made clear that freedom of expression does not have presumptive priority over other Convention rights. This is a consequence of s 3 of the Human Rights Act which requires all legislation to 'be read and given effect in a way which is compatible with the Convention rights'. See the Supplement to para 7.35 above.   **7.39**

The Court of Appeal in *Cream Holdings v Banerjee* may open up the opportunity to challenge the rule in *Bonnard v Perryman* in cases where the threatened publication is of defamatory information bearing on a personal and private aspect of the claimant's life. In *Cream Holdings* Sedley LJ said that if the threatened publication had not been essentially true the action would be in defamation: [88]. This need not necessarily be so. The cause of action for breach of confidence depends on the nature of the information itself and not on whether the information is true or false. When considering privacy rights it is arguably irrelevant whether the information is true or false. See the Main Work, paras 6.13, 10.18(3) n52.   **7.42**

(d) The claimant's choice

In *Cream Holdings v Banerjee* [2003] 2 All ER 318 the Court of Appeal has characterised the principles to be applied where an interim injunction is sought for breach of confidence or invasion of privacy as more stringent than *American Cyanamid* principles, see the Supplement to paras 7.35 and 7.36 above. The conflict between the principles established in *Cream Holdings* and the rule in *Bonnard v Perryman* nonetheless remains stark. *Cumpana and Mazare v Romania*, Application no 33348/96, judgment of 10 June 2003 (see the Supplement to   **7.44** paras 7.27 and 7.35) was not concerned with a prior restraint injunction, but does suggest that a false statement can be an interference with a person's private and family life. The anomalous situation in which the courts would restrain the publication of private information if the claimant said it was true, but not if the claimant said it was false, might be avoided by the privacy claimant not saying whether the information is true or false. This may be a perfectly legitimate stance: see the Supplement to para 7.42 above and the Main Work at paras 6.13 and 10.18(3) n52. The risk for the claimant is that, if the privacy injunction is refused, others may assume that the information was true because the action was not brought in defamation. A claim in defamation could be added by later amendment.

(e) A principled approach

7.47 In *Campbell v MGN Ltd* [2003] QB 633 the Court of Appeal noted at [29]–[31] that the claimant did not attempt to base her case on intrusion, and considered that concession in the light of *Letang v Cooper* [1965] 1 QB 232. The Court of Appeal concluded that the effect of the concession limited the scope of the legal argument. The passage appears to support the view that, without such a concession, the legal argument could have extended to other possible causes of action, such as intrusion or harassment, or defamation.

7.48 While allowing the appeal from the award of summary judgment, the Court of Appeal expressed a similar view: *Campbell v Frisbee* [2003] EMLR 76, [34].

7.50–7.52 For the principles now to be applied when a court is considering whether to restrain publication before trial, and for a discussion of these, see *Cream Holdings v Banerjee* [2002] 2 All ER 318 and the Supplement to paras 7.35–7.36, 7.39 and 7.42 above. If a claimant were now to seek a privacy injunction to prevent the publication of false and defamatory allegations bearing on his private life, thereby engaging a Convention right under Article 8 in place of or in addition to the right to protect his reputation, this would bring the long-standing rule in *Bonnard v Perryman* in direct conflict with the principles established in *Cream Holdings*. It is yet to be seen how the court will resolve this conflict: whether it will develop new principles that have regard to rights of privacy in relation to information which is both private and defamatory or whether the firmly entrenched rule against prior restraint embodied in *Bonnard v Perryman* will prevail in such cases.

E. French Law of Privacy and Defamation

7.65 n123 Two recent cases have confirmed that the right under the new article 9 of the Civil Code, stressing as it does the importance of the preservation of human dignity, extends to considerations of a person's rights after their death (ie the dignity of the corpse) as well as to the deceased's family's rights (ie the protection of the family's feelings and their right to grieve privately). Thus, two magazines which published photographs of the mutilated corpse of the Corsican Prefect, Mr Erignac, lying in the street in Ajaccio, shortly after he had been murdered on 6 February 1998, were found to be in breach of article 9 (*Cass 1re civ 20 dec 2000, D 2001*, 885, as cited in *Le Dalloz*, 2001, no11, 872ff). In another case, the makers of a film were found to have breached article 9 and were ordered to pay FF150,000 to the surviving child, when they made a film without her permission, based on the real life story of how some years earlier her divorced father staged a siege, locking himself and his three children up (including the claimant) for two weeks in his home, before shooting one policeman, and killing two of his children, and finally turning the gun on himself (*Cour d'appel de Paris (1re Ch B) 14 November 2002, Consorts Enrico et Grumberg c/C.Fourquet*). See also C Dupre, *Developing Key Privacy Rights*, M Colvin (ed) (2002) 63–65 and the Supplement to para 4.55 above.

8

PRIVACY, COPYRIGHT, AND MORAL RIGHTS

B. Privacy Interests and Copyright Subject Matter

(1) Types of Subject Matter

n24 See also section F below.   **8.16**

(4) Exclusive Rights

On 31 October 2003 the Copyright and Related Rights Regulations 2003 (SI   **8.25**
2003/2498) came into effect, implementing Directive 2001/29/EC on the
Harmonisation of Certain Aspects of Copyright and Related Rights in the
Information Society. The distinction between a 'broadcast' and a 'cable programme service' has been removed. Subject to exceptions, both types of transmission are now a 'broadcast': reg 4 (replacing s 6(1) CDPA and introducing a new s
6(1A)). A new right of 'making available to the public' has also been introduced
with respect to 'on-demand' services, although the place of occurrence of that restricted act has not been identified: reg 6(1) (introducing a new s 20 CDPA).

Some internet services are brought within the extended definition of 'broadcast' under s 6(1A). The restricted acts of broadcasting and making available to the public have become aspects of the right of 'communication to the public': reg 6(1) (introducing s 20(2) CDPA).

C. The Limitations on Exclusive Rights for News Reporting and Other Publication

(1) The 'Fair Dealing' Exception

8.35 Section 30 of the CDPA 1988 has been amended by SI 2003/2498 which implements the Copyright and Related Rights in the Information Society Directive 2001/29/EC as to which see the Supplement to para 8.25 above. The new s 30 provides as follows (the amendments are in italics):

(1) Fair dealing with a work for the purpose of criticism or review, of that or another work or of a performance of a work, does not infringe any copyright in the work provided that it is accompanied by a sufficient acknowledgement *and provided that the work has been made available to the public.*

(1A) *For the purposes of subsection (1) a work has been made available to the public if it has been made available by any means, including—*
(a) *the issue of copies to the public;*
(b) *making the work available by means of an electronic retrieval system;*
(c) *the rental or lending of copies of the work to the public;*
(d) *the performance, exhibition, playing or showing of the work in public;*
(e) *the communication to the public of the work;*
but in determining generally for the purposes of that subsection whether a work has been made available to the public no account shall be taken of any unauthorised act.

[Subsection (2) is not amended]

(3) No acknowledgement is required in connection with the reporting of current events by means of a sound recording, film *or broadcast where this would be impossible for reasons of practicality or otherwise.*

It should be noted that the amendment to subsection (3) differs from the Directive, art 5.3(c), which permits an exception for current events 'as long as the source including the author's name, is indicated, unless this turns out to be impossible'. The Directive does not specify 'for reasons of practicality or otherwise'.

The changes to s 30(1) and the insertion of s 30(1A) arise because art 5.3(c), (d) of the Directive requires that the fair dealing exception for criticism and review be limited to works already published. The requirements of the Directive mean that there will be no exception for criticism or review of an unpublished work. There may be rare circumstances in which these restrictions could infringe Article 10

ECHR and consideration will have to be given as to whether or not the court could or indeed should either refuse any injunction sought or apply the defence of public interest preserved by s 171(3): see *Church of Scientology et al v XS4all*, Dutch Court of Appeals 4 September 2003; *Re Quotation of News Pictures* [2002] ECC 20 (Austria) referred to in the Supplement to para 8.60 below and generally paras 8.54– 8.62 of the Main Work.

(c) Fair dealing

(ii) Unpublished works

See the Supplement to para 8.35 above. **8.45–8.47**

(iii) The amount and importance of the work taken

n90 Compare the approach of the Court of Appeal in *Campbell v MGN Ltd* **8.49** [2003] QB 633, CA [62]–[64] in which the Court held that if the disclosure of the central fact of the claimant's drug addiction was justifiable then 'the journalist must be given reasonable latitude as to the manner in which that information is conveyed to the public or his Article 10 right to freedom of expression will be unnecessarily inhibited'.

(2) The Public Interest Exception

See the Supplement to para 8.35 above. **8.57**

n111 See also the Supplement to para 8.49 n90 above. **8.60**

See also *Re Quotation of News Pictures* [2002] ECC 20 (Supreme Ct, Austria) where the Austrian statute did not specifically recognise a right to 'quote' photographs and this was held to be a *lacuna* contrary to freedom of speech which the Court would fill. A weekly newspaper published five miniaturised pages of the front page of the plaintiff's newspaper (including the photographs) in the context of an article about the plaintiff newspaper's attitude to a political group. There was reference in particular to an incident in which a photograph had been published of a youth suspected of arson in respect of which the plaintiff had not attempted to conceal the youth's identity. The plaintiff newspaper owned the copyright in the photograph and sought an injunction. The Austrian Copyright statute recognised a right to quote text but was silent as to photographs. The Court held that the statute failed to recognise that it might be just as necessary in the interest of freedom of speech to quote a picture as to quote language. The use of the photographs was also held to be justified in the context of the matters reported.

(3) Interviews and Section 58, CDPA

n114 See also *Gormley v EMI Records (Ireland) Ltd* [2000] ECC 370 (Supreme Ct, **8.63** Ireland) (sound recording of a pupil re-telling a bible story). The pupil's contention that she owned copyright in the sound recording as a literary work failed. The Irish statute provided that a literary work was made when it was 'first reduced to writing or some other material form'. The Court held that 'other material form' meant a symbol or notation which could be capable, without more, of being understood and this was not the case with a magnetic trace on a sound recording.

The following paragraphs are added to the end of the Main Work:

F. Databases

8.87 This Section considers the special treatment of databases pursuant to the European Parliament and Council Directive (96/9/EC) of 11 March 1996 on the Legal Protection of Databases (the 'Database Directive') and the potential impact of the Database Directive in the field of privacy and the media. The Directive was implemented in the UK by the Copyright and Rights in Databases Regulations 1997 (SI 1997/3032). In the only UK case concerning the new database right Laddie J ignored the Regulations and based his decision on the Directive itself: *British Horseracing Board and Others v William Hill Organization Ltd* [2001] RPC 612. There was no demurral from this approach by the Court of Appeal, which will be adopted in this section: *British Horseracing Board v William Hill Organization Ltd* [2002] ECC 24. The Court of Appeal referred the crucial questions on the appeal to the ECJ. No ruling has been given by the ECJ as of November 2003.

(1) The Database Directive

8.88 The Database Directive seeks to harmonise the protection given to databases across Member States, and introduces a new stand-alone *sui generis* database right. A database may be protected both by copyright and by database right. A database is defined as a collection of independent works, data, or other materials arranged in a systematic or methodical way and individually accessible by electronic or other means. The provisions of the Directive do not apply to computer programs used in the making or operation of databases accessible by electronic means: EP and Council Directive (96/9/EC) art 1.

8.89 If by reason of the selection and arrangement of its contents, a database constitutes 'the author's own intellectual creation' (Directive (96/9/EC) art 3(1)) then it will enjoy copyright protection as a literary work (CDPA s 3(1)(a)) with the same regime of exclusive rights and permitted acts as set out earlier in this chapter. It is unclear how, if at all, this differs from the CDPA 1988 requirement of originality. The new qualifying criteria for copyright do not apply to databases created before 27 March 1996 which will continue to enjoy copyright protection if they satisfy the usual originality requirements: Copyright and Related Rights in Databases Regulations 1997 (SI 1997/3032) reg 29.

The primary innovation in the Database Directive is the creation of a new data-   **8.90**
base right which applies irrespective of whether the database or any of its contents
qualify for copyright protection. This right subsists if there has been a substantial
investment in the obtaining, verification, or presentation of the contents of the
database. Investment includes any investment, whether of human, financial, or
technical resources: Copyright and Related Rights in Databases Regulations 1997
(SI 1997/3032) reg 12(1). It gives the maker of the database the right to prevent
extraction or re-utilisation of the whole or a substantial part of the database
(Directive (96/9/EC) art 7(1)) and also the repeated and systematic extraction or
re-utilisation of insubstantial parts of the database if such use unreasonably prej-
udices the legitimate interests of the maker: Directive (96/9/EC) art 7(5). The
database right applies to databases whenever made: Copyright and Related Rights
in Databases Regulations 1997 (SI 1997/3032) reg 27. In the *William Hill* case
Laddie J held that a database which was revised over time could nevertheless be regarded as one, evolving, database so that the taking of insubstantial parts of it over
time could be relied on by the rightholder, even though the database from which
the insubstantial part was taken was slightly different in each case.

'Extraction' is defined in the Directive as the permanent or temporary transfer of   **8.91**
all or a substantial part of the contents of a database to another medium. 'Re-utilisation' is defined as making available to the public all or a substantial part of the
contents of a database by the distribution of copies, by renting, or by on-line or
other forms of transmission: Copyright and Related Rights in Databases
Regulations 1997 (SI 1997/3032) reg 27.

The database right lasts for 15 years from the end of the calendar year in which the   **8.92**
database was completed or if made available to the public within that period for
15 years from the end of the calendar year in which it was first made available to
the public. Any substantial change to the database results in restarting of the 15-
year period: Directive (96/9/EC) art 10. The right applies to databases whose
makers or rightholders, if individuals, are nationals of or resident in Member
States, or if corporate are incorporated or have their principal place of business in
a Member State: Directive (96/9/EC) art 11. There are limited permitted acts allowing (a) extraction for private purposes of the contents of a non-electronic database, (b) extraction for the purposes of illustration for teaching or scientific
research to the extent justified by the non-commercial purpose as long as the
source is indicated, and (c) extraction or re-utilisation for the purposes of public
security or an administration or judicial procedure: Directive (96/9/EC) art 9.

(2) Privacy Considerations

The width of the definition of a database in the Directive and the Regulations   **8.93**
means that it is likely that collections of private correspondence, photograph al-
bums, address books, or the collection of entries in personal diaries and some

other collections of biographical detail or other historical fact could qualify for protection as databases. Clearly it also includes a wide range of commercially confidential collections of data.

8.94   In *British Horseracing Board v William Hill Organization Ltd* [2001] RPC 612 at first instance, Laddie J held that the database right is capable of protecting the *information* contained within the database from unauthorised use. This is a significant advance on the protection given by copyright to the form and structure of the database. He held that what is protected is the investment which went into obtaining, verifying, or presenting the contents of the database. An extraction or re-utilisation of those contents, even if the facts are then used for different purposes or presented in a wholly different manner, takes unfair advantage of that investment. The Court rejected the contention that acts which do not take advantage of the arrangement of the contents of the database or the way in which the maker of the database has made the contents individually accessible (what was described as the 'database-ness' of the collection of information) are not infringing acts. Laddie J stated at [78] that 'database rights protect the unlicensed taking and use of information'. The Court of Appeal has referred this question to the European Court of Justice, Peter Gibson LJ, giving the judgment of the Court, stating that if it had not been otherwise appropriate to make a reference, the Court would have probably upheld the conclusions of Laddie J. The three other questions referred to the ECJ by the Court of Appeal all went to the extent of the protection granted by the database right, including the question whether the restricted act of 're-utilisation' applied once the protected material had been previously published: *British Horseracing Board v William Hill Organization Ltd* [2002] ECC 24, at [41], [46]. Section 3(1), Human Rights Act 1998 requires the English courts, as far as possible, to read and give effect to subordinate legislation in a manner compatible with Convention rights. Thus, the extent of the rights created by the Regulations should arguably be 'read down', as appropriate, to avoid any inconsistency with Article 10 rights. For the effect of ECHR law in Community law see para 5.05 of the Main Work and the Supplement thereto.

8.95   The protection given by the database right is apparently stronger than that given by copyright for the further reason that the permitted acts in the Directive are much narrower than those in the CDPA 1988, and are exhaustive. There is no provision in the Directive for fair dealing for the purposes of reporting current events, nor for criticism or review. There is no express provision for the preservation of public interest 'defences', unlike the position for copyright infringement: s 171(3), CDPA. However, in appropriate circumstances Article 10 rights (if not public interest 'defences' at common law) would operate to counterbalance the enforcement of database rights: See *Lion Laboratories v Evans* [1985] 2 QB 525, CA; *Ashdown v Telegraph Group Ltd* [2002] Ch 149, CA.

9

JUSTIFICATIONS AND DEFENCES

B. Defences of General Application: Consent, Estoppel, Change of Position

n2 See too *Douglas v Hello! Ltd* [2003] 3 All ER 996.   **9.04**

(1) Consent

Note that the burden is not always on the defendant to prove consent: see Main   **9.06**
Work para 9.05 n4.

The point made in the last sentence of this paragraph was reiterated by Lindsay J   **9.07**
in *Douglas v Hello! Ltd*. He held that there had been an intrusion into the private

99

lives of the individuals concerned without consent according to the PCC Code and that, 'the very same principle in the Code that provides that the use of long lenses to take pictures of people in private places without their consent was unacceptable must, as I read it, inescapably also make the use of short lenses to take pictures of people in private places without their consent at least equally unacceptable': [186(vi)–(viii)], [202]–[205].

(c) What amounts to consent

9.09   This paragraph concerns the mode of consent.

9.10–9.13   These paragraphs deal with the extent of consent.

It must also be considered whether there are any factors which vitiate the validity of consent. It follows from general principles that even where actual consent is established, and applies to the particular publication, consent may be vitiated by misrepresentation, mistake, undue influence, or other factors which would vitiate a contractual agreement or other allegedly consensual arrangement. Consent orders can be set aside if entered into under a mutual mistake of fact, or in ignorance of a material fact, if the mistake would justify the setting aside of an agreement on the same ground (see *Chitty* (28th edn, 1999), para 5-090) or if the consent order was based on an agreement that was induced by misrepresentation (see *Chitty*, para 6-111). Similarly, consent induced by fraud, where the misapprehension of the consenting party goes to the root of the whole transaction, will be vitiated (see *Clerk & Lindsell* (18th edn, 2000), para 13-10) and consent will not afford a defence if the will of the consenting party was overcome by force or the fear of violence (see *Clerk & Lindsell*, para 13-11).

(f) Consent in the media privacy codes

9.20   n67 See too Ms Everitt and Mr. Brick and the *Welwyn and Hatfield Times*, 27 January 2003 (Report 61).

C. Waiver of Rights

9.29–9.33   The issue of the extent to which a person waives his or her right to privacy by publishing his or her own private affairs was raised in *Campbell v MGN Ltd* [2003] QB 633, CA, *Campbell v Frisbee* [2003] EMLR 76, CA, *Douglas v Hello! Ltd* and *Lady Archer v Williams* [2003] FSR 869.

The simple fact that an individual has achieved prominence on the public stage does not mean that his or her private life can be laid bare by the media, but if that person chooses to make untrue pronouncements about his or her private life, the press will normally be entitled to put the record straight (see *Campbell v MGN Ltd* at [41], [43]). See also the Supplement to para 9.80 below.

In *Campbell v Frisbee* at [22] the Court of Appeal considered that the proposition that a duty of confidentiality expressly assumed under contract should carry more weight when balanced against the right to freedom of expression was arguable but noted that the effects on that duty when the contract was wrongfully repudiated were not clearly established. At [34] Lord Phillips MR referred to Lightman J's dismissal of *Woodward v Hutchins* [1977] 1 WLR 760, CA, and while observing that the judge at first instance may well have been correct, held that summary judgment ought not to have been granted in the claimant's favour, as on its face it lent support to the proposed defence.

In *Douglas v Hello! Ltd* the submission that *Woodward and Hutchins* was authority for the proposition that an individual who has sought publicity loses the right to insist upon confidentiality in respect of publicity was rejected by Lindsay J as going too far [225]. He found that the case illustrated that where a claimant has fostered an image which is not a true one, there can be a public interest in correcting it.

In *Lady Archer v Williams* at [64]–[66] Jackson J distinguished the claimant's position from that of the footballer in *A v B plc* and held that neither the claimant's role in society nor the fact that she had discussed aspects of her private life on TV and in a radio programme made her a person whose way of life or activities 'generated legitimate public interest in any of the matters which the defendant is seeking to publicise'. Those matters were said to 'fall very low in the scale of public interest': [61]. The judge did not refer to *Woodward v Hutchins*, but, as this last citation indicates, approached the issue as one of public interest rather than of waiver. As to the public interest in this context see paras 9.59, 9.82–9.84, and 10.64–10.65 of the Main Work and of the Supplement thereto, below.

Although not concerned with personal information it is worthy of note that in *Jockey Club v Buffham* [2003] QB 462, Gray J held that a factor weighing in favour of permitting publication (but of itself not sufficient to justify denying the claimant's rights of confidence) was the fact that the Jockey Club had placed relevant material in the public domain: [57(v)].

n93 See too *Ashworth Hospital v MGN Ltd* [2002] 1 WLR 2033, HL *per* Lord Woolf CJ at [32].

n96 In *Douglas v Hello! Ltd*, Lindsay J found that the claimants had a right to commercial confidence and to control the publicity coverage of their wedding. In so finding, he regarded the claimants' position as akin to that of holders of a trade secret: [227]–[228]. **9.33**

9.35 In the *Attard* case the parents of Gracie, the survivor of conjoined twins, applied successfully to discharge the injunction which prevented her identification, so that they could sell to the media information about and pictures of Gracie. The *Manchester Evening News* obtained photographs of Gracie, taken outside the hospital. The parents then successfully applied for an injunction preventing publication without their consent: *Attard v Greater Manchester Newspapers Ltd* (Fam, 124/15 June 2001). In the light of this decision of the court, the PCC declined to adjudicate under clause 3 of the Code (Privacy). But it rejected all other complaints, drawing attention to the fact that the Code, mirroring exactly the terms of s 12(4) of the Human Rights Act, specifically charges the PCC with having regard to the extent to which the material has, or is about to, become available to the public with the consent of the complainants, as was clearly the case in that instance. In its adjudication, the PCC said that a complainant who releases or sells information or photographs may become disentitled to the protection of the Code: 'Privacy is—in the Commission's opinion—not a commodity which can be sold on one person's terms:' Messrs Pannone on behalf of Michaelangelo and Rina Attard and *The Manchester Evening News*, 15 June 2001 (Report 55).

In *Douglas v Hello! Ltd*, the *Hello!* defendants argued (along the lines of the PCC's approach in *Attard*) that a personal privacy right evaporated or was waived upon sale for publication, on the footing that such a sale is inconsistent with the maintenance or protection of personal privacy. It was argued that this approach is bolstered by the reference in s 12(4), HRA to the relevance of the fact that the material has or is about to become available to the public. Lindsay J rejected this argument, stating that s 12(4) of the HRA does not support this approach, even as regards a personal or individual confidence: [210]. It was inevitable that the waiver argument would fail, once Lindsay J approached *Douglas v Hello! Ltd*, as he did, as a case of the sale of a commercial confidence or trade secret: [195]–[196], [210], since the sale of a trade secret is plainly not inconsistent with the preservation of confidence. Lindsay J's approach allows, at least in some cases—in particular a celebrity wedding held in private—a personal confidence to be converted into a commercial one by sale.

The characterisation of the claimants' rights as being in the nature of a trade secret raises the question why the Court of Appeal considered that the sale of the rights rendered the claims to be less deserving of an injunction on that ground. Lindsay J (at [271]) considered it plain that there were arguments that could have been presented to the Court of Appeal to do otherwise than discharge the interim injunction. He noted that in the Court of Appeal the argument in relation to confidentiality was put primarily in a privacy rather than in a commercial context. He also noted that it was not urged on the Court of Appeal that by refusing the injunction because damages sufficed, the Court of Appeal would, in effect, be allowing a compulsory purchase by *Hello!* of a right to breach exclusiveness for which its trade rival had paid so much. That was despite the Court of Appeal regarding the claimants as having a sound claim in confidence. He also noted that the Court of Appeal took a different view on the test of likelihood to be applied under s 12, HRA to that more recently adopted by the Court of Appeal in *Cream Holdings Ltd v Banerjee* [2003] 2 All ER 318.

9.36 n104 See now also the Court of Appeal's judgment in *Campbell v MGN Ltd* at [41] and the Supplement to paras 9.82–9.84 below.

9.37 See too Bernie Ecclestone and *The Mail on Sunday*, 25 August 2002 (Report 60).

9.38 On 'compromising' privacy, see also Pumfrey J's *obiter* observations in *Notts Healthcare Trust v News Group Newspapers Ltd* [2002] EMLR 709 at [55], that 'it might plausibly be said' that the prisoner, A, may have 'compromised' any right to privacy in a photographic image of him by his conduct in inviting use in the media of another, different photograph of him.

Contrast the position where a claimant, after his identity has been disclosed without his consent, courts publicity to draw attention to his plight. In *Peck v UK* (2003) 36 EHRR 41 the ECtHR held that the applicant's subsequent appearances in the media did not diminish the serious nature of the interference or reduce the correlative requirement of care concerning disclosures. 'The applicant was the victim of a serious interference with his right to privacy involving national and local media coverage: it cannot therefore be held against him that he sought thereafter to avail himself of the media to expose and complain about that wrongdoing': [86]. In so holding the Court appeared to accept the applicant's submission that he faced 'the classic dilemma of one whose privacy has been interfered with: seeking a remedy and defending one's position by speaking out inevitably leads to further publicity': [75]. Mr Peck had participated in one national radio programme, appeared on three national television programmes and had consented to his name or photograph appearing in numerous newspaper articles about his case in the months after the events which gave rise to his complaint: [23]. See too *Ashworth Hospital Authority v MGN Ltd* [2001] 1 WLR 515, CA, *per* Lord Phillips MR at [49–54]. In the light of *A v B plc* [2003] QB 195, CA, decisions of the PCC (as opposed to the provisions of the Code) are not a legitimate source of authority on applications for interim injunctions (*per* Lord Woolf CJ at 11(xv)).

D. Defences to Intrusive Acts

(2) Cases Where the Media Have or May Have Special Defences

9.42 n114 The Court of Appeal in *Campbell v MGN Ltd* has now held that the media exemption under s 32, Data Protection Act 1998 applies to publication as well as pre-publication activities: see the Supplement to para 5.80 above.

E. Defences to Claims for Disclosure of Private Facts

9.47 In addition to those defences discussed in this Section of the Main Work, a number of other justifications for what would otherwise be breaches of confidence or privacy have been identified in the authorities and in reports on the law of confidence and privacy. These are briefly described below.

(a) Innocence

In the law of confidence the position of a third party who acquires and uses confidential information provided by another depends on his state of knowledge. An 'innocent' party, who uses information in ignorance of the fact that it is another's confidential information may not be liable to pay damages (*Valeo Vision SA v Flexible Lamps Ltd* [1995] RPC 205) although he may be liable to an injunction once on notice, subject to defences of *bona fide* purchase or change of position (see the discussion in R G Toulson & C M Phipps, *Confidentiality* (1996) paras 7-02 to 7-09). Draft bills to afford rights of privacy in England and Wales put forward in 1987 and 1989 both included a defence that the defendant, having taken all reasonable care, neither knew nor intended that his conduct would constitute a breach of privacy: see the Calcutt Report, *Report of the Committee on Privacy and Related Matters* Cm 1102 June 1990, Appendix J cl 3(a) and Appendix K cl 3(a). However, now that liability for breach of confidence or privacy in relation to personal information is coming to be defined by reference to what the defendant knows or ought to know (*A v B plc* at [11](ix)) it would seem that there may be no need for such a defence.

Note also in this context Lord Hoffmann's remarks in *Wainwright v Home Office* [2003] 3 WLR 1137 [51] that 'it is one thing to wander carelessly into the wrong hotel bedroom and another to hide in the wardrobe to take photographs'. However, his observation in the same paragraph that Article 8 may not require a monetary remedy for a merely negligent act is not consistent with Strasbourg jurisprudence. See para 1.68 above. It is generally unnecessary to establish any particular state of mind in respect of a breach of the Convention, but the conduct of the parties as a whole (including whether the acts which are alleged to give rise to the violation were deliberate or accidental) may be taken into account in determining the gravity of the interference.

(b) Lawful authority

Disclosure by compulsion of law was one of the exceptions to the banker's duty of secrecy identified by the Court of Appeal in *Tournier v National Provincial and Union Bank of England* [1924] 1 KB 461, 473, and see *Toulson & Phipps* para 3-15. A defence of lawful authority was envisaged by the Calcutt

Committee, and had been provided for in the draft bills mentioned above: see the Calcutt Report (above) at para 12.19(e) and Appendix J cl 3(f), and Appendix K cl 3(e). It is not common for the media to be compelled or authorised by law to disclose personal information, but orders for disclosure of sources and the provisions of the Police and Criminal Evidence Act 1984, Terrorism Act 2000 and Official Secrets Act 1989 are examples of situations where this may occur (see the Main Work paras 1.30–1.31 and Chapter 14 generally).

(c) Protection of self or property

Disclosure where the disclosing party's interests require it is a further exception to the banker's duty of secrecy identified in *Tournier* and is of general application in the law of confidence: see *Toulson & Phipps* para 3-17. A defence to this effect was included in each of the draft bills mentioned above: see the Calcutt Report Appendix J cl 3(d) and Appendix K cl 3(c). Such a defence might be of relevance in a media case where, for example, a newspaper or broadcaster needed to use confidential information in order to mount a defence of justification to a libel claim against it. Where the defence does not succeed, improperly obtained evidence may be admitted. In *Jones v University of Warwick* [2003] 1 WLR 954 a defendant was permitted to adduce evidence improperly obtained by trespass and infringement of the claimant's Article 8 rights, because it is in the public interest that truth should be revealed in litigation (in that case a personal injury claim). The Court of Appeal indicated that the trial court could have reflected its disapproval of the insurer's improper and unjustified conduct by the costs order which it made. The claimant might also have brought a claim for damages in trespass. The claim would be comparable to the claim on the cross-undertaking in damages brought by the defendant to an improper search and seizure order in *Columbia Pictures v Robinson* [1987] Ch 38, 88. Scott J awarded a total of £10,000, £7,000 of which recognised the 'contumely and affront' to Mr Robinson.

(d) Publication would be protected by privilege if defamatory

In US law a 'private facts' claim may be met by defences of absolute and qualified privilege; similarly in South Africa: see Main Work para 9.117. A defence that, if the action had been brought in defamation, privilege would have applied was identified as a candidate defence to a privacy claim by the Calcutt Committee: see its Report at para 12.19(b), and see also the draft privacy bills at Appendix J cl.3(e) and Appendix K cl.3(d). At paras 9.107 and 9.117–9.119 of the Main Work it was suggested that such a defence might be developed in English law. However, the Court of Appeal in *Campbell v MGN Ltd* has now rejected such an approach: see the Supplement to paras 9.60, 9.90 above and 9.117 below.

(1) Facts in the Public Domain

9.48   It is arguable that there exists a principle, distinct from the public domain doctrine, that information which is a matter of public record will not be protected from disclosure on the grounds of confidentiality (see the Supplement to para 6.102 above).

(2) Breach of Confidence: the Public Interest and the Rights of Others

(a) **Introduction**

9.53   This does not mean that Article 10 rights are to be given priority over Article 8 rights: see *Douglas v Hello! Ltd* [2001] QB 967, at [135] *per* Sedley LJ, and [2003] 3 All ER 996, *per* Lindsay J at 186 (v). See also para 6.152 of the Main Work n 477 and the Supplement thereto and G Phillipson, 'Transforming Breach of Confidence? Towards a Common Law Right of Privacy under the Human Rights Act' [2003] 66:5 MLR 726, 748–58.

9.54   n136 See too *X and Y v News Group Newspapers and MGN Ltd* [2003] FSR 850 where Butler-Sloss P granted life-long, world-wide anonymity to Mary Bell and her daughter on the ground that there was a serious risk that the Article 8 rights of Mary Bell would be breached if there were public disclosure of their new identities and addresses.

The BBC won its appeal against the finding of the Court of Appeal that it had breached Article 10 by refusing to broadcast the ProLife party election broadcast: [2003] 2 WLR 1403. The House of Lords held that the Court of Appeal had asked itself the wrong question: 'It treated the case as if it concerned the primary right not to be prevented from expressing one's political views and concluded that questions of taste and decency were not an adequate ground for censorship. The real issue in the case is whether the requirements of taste and decency are a discriminatory, arbitrary or unreasonable condition for allowing a political party free access at election time to a particular medium, namely television' *per* Lord Hoffmann at [62]. Thus the right in question is not 'a right not to be prevented from expressing one's opinions' but 'a right to fair consideration for being afforded the opportunity to do so' [58].

For reputation as a Convention right, see the Supplement to para 2.13 above.

In *Re B (Children: Patient Confidentiality)* [2003] 2 FLR 813, CA it was held that a psychiatrist who received confidential information from a patient which gave rise to concern as to abuse in respect of the patient's young sisters would have to strike a balance between the importance of preserving patient confidentiality and the protection of those children. For a fuller discussion of professional confidentiality see R Pattenden, *The Law of Professional–Client Confidentiality* (2003).

This aspect of the judgment of the Court of Appeal in *A v B plc* was explained in **9.59**
Campbell v MGN Ltd at [39]–[43]. See further the Supplement to paras 9.65 and
9.82–9.84 below. For a critique of this explanation see G Phillipson, 'Judicial
Reasoning in Breach of Confidence cases under the Human Rights Act: not taking privacy seriously?' [2003] EHRLR Special Issue 54, 63.

The indications from the judgment of the Court of Appeal in *Campbell v MGN Ltd* **9.60**
are that the courts may be reluctant to introduce concepts from other privacy rights
based on different causes of action. The Court held that the latitude given to statements published on an occasion of qualified privilege should not be imported into
public interest defences in breach of confidence claims to enforce privacy interests,
even though this solution had been adopted by the American and South African
courts in connection with the tort of breach of privacy (see at [59]–[62] *per* Lord
Phillips MR). A latitude should be given to the media, but on Article 10 grounds
connected with journalistic credibility: see the Supplement to para 9.90 below.

n157 See now also the Court of Appeal judgment in *Campbell v Frisbee*. **9.64**

(b) The Types of Information Relevant to a Public Interest Defence

See the Supplement to paras 9.82–9.84 below. **9.65**

(i) *Wrongdoing*

See *Istil Group Inc v Zahoor* [2003] 2 All ER 252 where an application for an in- **9.68**
junction to prevent reliance on certain documents on grounds of confidentiality
was not granted because the equitable jurisdiction to restrain breach of confidence
gave way to the public interest in the disclosure of wrongdoing (in that case the
judge found there had been forgery and misleading evidence) and the proper administration of justice.

n173 See also the criticism of *Woodwards v Hutchins* in *Campbell v Frisbee* at [34].

(ii) *Purposes beneficial to the community*

Other public welfare policies. Disclosure of the identity of an employee who **9.73–9.78**
had breached his duty of confidentiality by supplying the medical records of a
convicted murderer to a newspaper was held to be justified both to protect the integrity of the hospital authority's records and to identify and punish the informant, see *Ashworth Hospital Authority v MGN Ltd* [2002] 1 WLR 2033, HL
(although not, after further delay, in *Mersey Care NHS Trust v Ackroyd* [2003] FSR
820). Disclosure of confidential documents revealing the existence or apparent
existence of widespread corruption within horse-racing was ordered because the
public interest in disclosure outweighed the right of confidence of the Jockey
Club; the court attached significance to the fact that the Jockey Club was a public
authority: *Jockey Club v Buffham* [2003] QB 462, at [57].

9.80 **Correcting the record.** In *Campbell v MGN Ltd* at [35]–[36] the Court of Appeal stressed the concessions which had been made on behalf of the claimant below. These included that the newspaper could legitimately report that the claimant had a drug problem and could put the record straight so as to give the lie to her untrue assertions to the media that she did not take drugs. The court appeared to indicate that this concession had been appropriately made. Giving the judgment of the Court, Lord Phillips MR stated at [43]:

> The courts are in the process of identifying, on a case by case basis, the principles by which the law of confidentiality must accommodate the Article 8 and the Article 10 rights. One principle, which has been recognised by the parties in this case, is that, where a public figure chooses to make untrue public pronouncements about his or her private life, the press will normally be entitled to put the record straight.

In *Campbell v Frisbee* the Court of Appeal allowed the defendant's appeal from the decision of Lightman J who had upheld an earlier order for summary judgment. The Court of Appeal held that (among other things) the defence of public interest was arguable. That defence was in part based on correcting the record (as in *Woodward v Hutchins*). It was that the claimant had painted a false picture of herself to the public, having (so it was said) falsely 're-branded' herself as a reformed and stable individual, evidenced by the fact that she was engaged to be married; whereas she was far from being reformed or stable and was carrying on an affair. Lord Phillips MR, giving the judgment of the Court, stated at [34] that 'Lightman J may well be right to suggest that *Woodward v Hutchins* should no longer be applied, but on its face it lends support to Miss Frisbee's proposed defence.'

In *Campbell v Frisbee* the Court further observed at [33]–[35] that in *Campbell v MGN Ltd* the claimant had largely resolved the conflict between Articles 8 and 10 by conceding that the defendants were entitled to put the record straight; but that in this case the tension between the two Articles still had to be resolved because the law was insufficiently clear. This may be contrasted with the approach of the Court in *Campbell v MGN Ltd* at [43].

n209 See now also the judgment of the Court of Appeal in *Campbell v MGN Ltd*.

n211 See now also the judgment of the Court of Appeal in *Campbell v Frisbee*.

9.81 See the Supplement to paras 9.82–9.84 below.

(iii) Information concerning public figures

9.82–9.84 In *Campbell v MGN Ltd* Lord Phillips MR, giving the judgment of the Court of Appeal, explained what the Court understood by this 'legitimate interest'. He stated (at [40]) that the fact that the public has 'an understandable and so a legitimate interest in being told' (*per* Lord Woolf) information about a public figure (even trivia) did not refer to:

private facts which a fair-minded person would consider it offensive to disclose. That is clear from his [ie Lord Woolf's] subsequent commendation of the guidance on striking a balance between Article 8 and Article 10 rights provided by the Council of Europe Resolution 1165 of 1998.

He went on to state at [41]:

For our part we would observe that the fact that an individual has achieved promi-nence on the public stage does not mean that his private life can be laid bare by the media. We do not see why it should necessarily be in the public interest that an in-dividual who has been adopted as a role model, without seeking this distinction, should be demonstrated to have feet of clay.

Subsequently, in *Lady Archer v Williams* the defendant was unsuccessful in an at-tempt to justify disclosure in reliance on the observations in *A v B plc* about 'pub-lic figures' and 'role models' : see the Supplement to paras 9.29–9.33 above.

In *Craxi (No 2) v Italy*, Application no 25337/94, judgment of 17 July 2003, [65], it was held that public figures are entitled to the enjoyment of the guarantees set out in Article 8 of the Convention on the same basis as every other person.

German law adopts an approach which is more consistent with the ECHR. In *Princess Caroline II*, BGH NJW 1996, 1128–9 (see para 6.77 of this Supplement) at para III.A.2(b), (c) it is expressed as follows (in a passage which merits citation at length):

(b) Pictures belonging to the sphere of contemporary history may, however, be dis-tributed or shown without permission of the person involved, unless legally pro-tected interests of the person depicted are thereby infringed (§ 23 I, No1, II KUG). Pictures of persons regarded as 'absolute contemporary persons' form part of con-temporary history. The plaintiff belongs to this group of persons . . . Decisive for the classification of a person as an absolute person of contemporary history is the fact that the public regards his pictures as important and worthy of note just because of the particular person shown. The public has a justified interest, based on a real need for information, in seeing pictures of these persons . . . As the eldest daughter of the reigning Prince of Monaco, the plaintiff belongs to this circle of persons as she, her-self, has acknowledged . . .

(c) There are, however, limits to the publication without permission of pictures of persons who form part of contemporary history. According to § 23 II KUG publi-cation is prohibited where the justified interests of the person shown outweigh the other interests at stake. Whether or not this is the case here, must be decided through a process of weighing up the various rights and interests involved so that in each individual case it is established whether the public interest in information pro-tected by the freedom of the press (art. 5 of the Constitution), which the defendant can cite as justification, has precedence over the plaintiff's right to her personality (Art. 2 GG) to which she refers . . .

(aa) The protection of a person's private sphere of life is of special importance when the two legal interests are weighed against each other. The right to respect one's own private sphere of life is an emanation of the general right to one's own personality, which grants every person an autonomous area of personal life within which he can develop and experience his own individuality, free from the interferences of others. The right to be left alone and 'to belong to oneself' forms part of this area (BVerfGE 34, 238, 245 et seq.; BVerfGE 35, 202, 220; for the right to be left alone as part of the right to privacy under American law see Katz v. United States 389 Supreme Court (1967), 347, 350 et seq.; Warren/Brandeis, 4 Harvard Law Review [1980] 193 et seq.; Götting Persönlichkeitsrechte als Vermögensrechte, 1995, 168 et seq., 174). As a result, since 1954, the German courts have, especially in the area of civil law consistently given particular weight to the right to respect one's own private sphere of life, i.e. treated it as a basic right, guaranteed by the constitution, which includes the right to one's own image . . .

(bb) The right to respect one's own sphere of private life can be claimed by anyone, and can therefore be claimed by the plaintiff, even if she is a person of contemporary history. For even such persons need not tolerate pictures which depict central aspects of their private life, for instance their domestic surroundings, being taken for later publication without their permission . . . Only in exceptional circumstances, can the distribution of pictures from this area be permissible, i.e. where an overriding public interest justifies such an intrusion . . .

(aa) Like anyone else, persons who are part of contemporary history have the right which must be respected by all third persons to retreat to places outside their own home where they wish to be alone or, at least, left secluded from the general public . . .

Note however, that whether the protection afforded to the 'central aspects' of the Princess's private life even under German law goes as far as Article 8 requires is to be determined by the European Court of Human Rights in a forthcoming judgment. See the Supplement to paras 1.79 and 2.59 n 131 above.

9.82   n217 See too *Douglas v Hello! Ltd* [2003] 3 All ER 996, at [186 (iii)].

(c) The extent and degree of disclosure in the public interest

(i) In what circumstances will disclosure to the public be appropriate?

9.85   n220 The Court of Appeal in *Campbell v MGN Ltd* declined to apply these authorities (*Jansen Van Vuuren* and *Bichler*) to defences to a claim for breach of confidence: see [59]–[64] and the Supplement to paras 9.90 and 9.117 below.

9.87   See too *Jockey Club v Buffham* [2003] QB 462, at [46]–[51] where Gray J applied the test of proportionality set out by Sedley LJ in *London Regional Transport v Mayor of London* [2003] EMLR 88 in holding that there existed matters of sufficient general interest concerning malpractice in horse-racing to warrant disclosure by the media of specified passages from the claimant's confidential documents. Documents relating to the integrity and fairness of bookmaking to the betting public fell within this category. The fact that the Jockey Club was investigating or bound to investigate the evidence of malpractice was not a justification for restraining disclosure to the public by the media, where what was in issue was not merely whether the regulator had been taking effective action, but that if effective action could not be taken, more effective means must be found to maintain the integrity of racing. Other factors taken into account by the judge included the fact that the confidential information revealed the existence or apparent existence of wide-scale corruption in racing, which itself was a matter of widespread public interest to those following or involved in the business of racing: [57].

(ii) How much disclosure is justified in the public interest?

In *X and Y v News Group Newspapers and MGN Ltd* [2003] FSR 850, Butler-Sloss **9.88** P held that there was sufficient information about Mary Bell and her daughter in the public domain for the press and other parts of the media to be able to comment freely on the relevant aspects of the case. Thus, there was no need to know the present name and address of Mary Bell or her daughter: [39], [60(2)].

In *Campbell v MGN Ltd* the Court of Appeal held that photographs of the **9.89** claimant in the street, having just left a therapy session at Narcotics Anonymous, were not protected by the law of confidence because they did not convey confidential information: see [30]–[34] and the Supplement to para 6.52 above. However, the photographs were arguably the fruits of a breach of confidence which, absent other considerations, might have given rise to a remedy. See also the Supplement to paras 2.25 and 6.52 and paras 2.28–2.34 of the Main Work.

The approach of the first instance judge in *Campbell v MGN Ltd*, referred to in **9.90** this paragraph, was reversed on appeal. The issue was whether the admitted entitlement in the public interest to publish the fact that the claimant was a drug addict and was receiving treatment justified publishing accompanying detail. At [59]–[64] the Court held, applying *Fressoz and Roire v France* [2001] EHRR 1, [54], that the detail was not such as to merit protection and that, in any event, it was part of a legitimate (even necessary) journalistic package which gave credibility to the newspaper's assertions that the claimant had portrayed a false image of herself. The Court declined to follow the approach taken in the USA and South Africa, based on the law of defamation (see the Supplement to para 9.60 above).

(d) The degree of proof necessary to establish public interest

In *Jockey Club v Buffham* [2003] QB 462, Gray J held that the burden of proof **9.92–9.95** lay on the Jockey Club to show that the BBC should be enjoined, notwithstanding that the BBC was not a party to the proceedings and had applied to the Court after it had been given notice of the injunction against the original defendant (and after a final order had been made).

F. Defences to 'False Light' Claims

(2) Data Protection

9.108 The Court of Appeal's decision in *Campbell v MGN Ltd* has affected the scope of the public interest defences discussed in paras 5.78–5.96 of the Main Work. See the Supplement to paras 5.80–5.90 above.

G. Defences to Appropriation of Name or Likeness Claims

9.110 The topic of controlling publicity was raised at trial in *Douglas v Hello! Ltd*. The defendants submitted that what Mr and Mrs Douglas were seeking was not privacy or confidentiality but control. Lindsay J stated that control was not an improper objective of confidence, and as such it did not deny the application of the law of confidence but was simply another factor in the overall balance between confidence and freedom of expression: [216].

n276 See also *Campbell v MGN Ltd* at [11], [30]–[34] where the Court of Appeal held that photographs of the claimant in the street could not be made the subject of a claim in confidence and recorded that the claimant's Counsel had abstained from pursuing any case that English law should recognise the wrong, recognised in some other jurisdictions, of publishing a photograph taken without consent. See also the Supplement to paras 2.25 and 6.52 above and paras 2.28–2.34 of the Main Work.

n278 The decision of Laddie J on liability in *Irvine v Talksport Ltd* was upheld on appeal: [2003] 2 All ER 881.

See also the Supplement to paras 8.25 and 8.35 above.

H. Commentary and Future Directions

(2) The Public Interest Defence

(a) Comparison with defamation

9.114 The decision in *Campbell v MGN Ltd* has thrown doubt on the view of Morland J that it would be absurd to refer to inaccuracies as removing the mark of confidentiality from the information. The Court of Appeal did not expressly deal with the subject but held at [57] that the fact that some of the information of which complaint was made was inaccurate strengthened the view that this was not a matter that required the intervention of the Court.

9.115 See the Supplement to para 9.117 below.

The question of whether the same test of public interest should apply to justify publication of confidential/private information and to the defence of qualified privilege to a claim for defamation was raised in *Campbell v MGN Ltd*. The Court of Appeal held at [61] that it should not:

> Both the South African and the American authorities were addressing a tort of breach of privacy. In this jurisdiction both protection of privacy by expanding the scope of breach of confidence and the public interest defence of qualified privilege in defamation are in the course of development—as to the latter see *Reynolds v The Times* [2001] 2 AC 127 and *Loutchansky v The Times* [2002] 1 All ER 652; [2002] 2 WLR 640. We do not believe that the same test of public interest applies to justify publication in these two very different torts.

See also the Supplement to paras 9.60 and 9.90 above.

The decision in *Campbell v MGN Ltd* suggests that the law relating to public interest in privacy/confidence and defamation claims is not going to develop on the same principles. The Court of Appeal noted at [61] that these were 'two very different torts' which were both in the course of development. See the Supplement to para 9.117 above. **9.118**

I. Limitation of Actions

n313 See now A McGee, *Limitation Periods* (4th edn, 2002). **9.128**

(1) Primary Limitation Periods

(a) Claims under the Data Protection Act 1998

n314 See A McGee, *Limitation Periods* (4th edn, 2002) at paras 11.002–11.006 and 11.011. **9.130**

(b) Breach of confidence

n316 See A McGee, *Limitation Periods* (4th edn, 2002) , para 10.002. **9.131**

n317 See A McGee, *Limitation Periods* (4th edn, 2002), paras 4.013, 4.022–4.024.

(e) Trespass to land, nuisance, breach of statutory duty, harassment, and wrongful interference with goods

n337 See A McGee, *Limitation Periods* (4th edn, 2002), para 5.003. **9.136**

(2) Special Cases

(a) Cases of personal injury or death

9.138   The effect of ss 11(4) and 11(5) Limitation Act 1980 as stated in this paragraph is that a shorter limitation period applies to a breach of confidence which causes injury or death than to one which merely injures feelings.

n346 This note does not apply to Scotland (see para 9.137 n338 of the Main Work).

(4) Breach of Privacy Committed Abroad

(d) Exceptions

9.148   n386 See A McGee, *Limitation Periods* (4th edn, 2002), paras 25.012–25.015.

10

REMEDIES

A. Introduction

n4 In *Campbell v MGN Ltd* [2003] QB 633, [127] the Court of Appeal re-iterated **10.01** that reference to parliamentary material under the principle of *Pepper v Hart* should be a last resort. The Court in that case did not consider s 32, Data Protection Act 1998 to be ambiguous or obscure, despite it being common ground between the parties that it was.

In *Wilson v First County Trust Ltd (No 2)* [2003] 3 WLR 568, [66], [139] the House of Lords said that the courts must be careful not to treat a ministerial statement as indicative of the objective intention of Parliament. Although the case concerned the circumstances in which it would be permissible to rely on parliamentary material to assess the compatibility of legislation with Convention rights (as to which see the Supplement to para 1.81 n 216 above) their Lordships' remarks were also directed at use of parliamentary material to resolve an ambiguity in legislation under the rule in *Pepper v Hart*: see Lord Nicholls at [58] and Lord Hobhouse at [139]. In summarising the current position, some doubt was cast on the precise scope of that rule. Lord Hope suggested at [113] that its purpose was to prevent the executive from placing a meaning on words used in legislation which is different from that which ministers attributed to those words when promoting the legislation in Parliament: *R v Secretary of State for the Environment, ex p Spath Holme Ltd* [2001] 2 AC 349, 407–8. Lord Hobhouse at [140], appearing sympathetic to this explanation, advocated against any extension of the rule or relaxation of the strict observation of the safeguards which it included. Lord Nicholls said at [60] that it was not necessary to decide whether *Pepper v Hart* did more than permit the courts, when ascertaining the intention of Parliament, to have regard to ministerial statements made in Parliament in the same way as they may have regard to ministerial statements made outside Parliament. The various observations do not sit easily together. If the purpose of the rule in *Pepper v Hart* is to prevent the executive from reneging on some sort of 'legitimate expectation' (*per* Lord Hobhouse at [140]) created by what it had previously said, then surely the only statements that are relevant are those of the minister or promoter of the Bill. This is the rationale for permitting reference to ministerial statements in Parliament where they are relevant to a challenge by way of judicial review of a decision the minister has taken: see, for example, *R v Secretary of State for the Home Department, ex p Brind* [1991] 1 AC 696. If, on the other hand, ministerial statements do not have a special status and must accord with the will of Parliament as a whole if their weight is to be determinative then the number of occasions when reference to Hansard will provide the necessary clarity to resolve an ambiguity in legislation will be even further curtailed. It is usually hard enough to find a clear and unambiguous explanation of the meaning of a statutory provision from the statements of the minister or promoter of the Bill, let alone from the debates of Parliament in their entirety. See also the Supplement to para 13.136 below.

B. Section 12, Human Rights Act 1998

(4) Section 12(3)

10.06 On how the courts have interpreted 'likely', and the exercise to be carried out when a court is considering both Article 8 and Article 10, see the Supplement to paras 7.35 above and 10.32–10.38 below.

10.06–10.07 In *Cream Holdings v Banerjee* [2003] 2 All ER 318 the Court of Appeal had regard to parliamentary material which it requested of the parties after the conclusion of the hearing in order to interpret s 12(3), HRA. The parties might be forgiven for not having provided that material at the hearing given previous statements by the Court of Appeal in *Douglas v Hello! Ltd* and courts in other interim injunction applications that the meaning of the section was clear. Be that as it may, the Court was referred to the Home Secretary's remarks at vol 315, col 536 of Hansard for 2 July 1998 but not to the passage from col 538 cited in para 10.06 of the Main Work comparing the position in Scots law. Had it been so the Court might have had more difficulty in reconciling the lower threshold test which it ultimately held applies ('real prospect of success') with the words of Lord Fraser in *NWL Ltd v Woods* [1979] 3 All ER 614, 628 cited at para 10.07 of the Main Work (incorporated by reference in the Home Secretary's allusion to the pre-HRA position in Scotland) that a party had to be 'very likely' to succeed at trial if it was to obtain interim relief.

C. Injunctions

(2) Interim Injunctions

(a) Preliminary considerations

(i) *Choice of cause of action*

In addition to the causes of action listed in this paragraph of the Main Work, there is a further jurisdiction when children are involved: see *Re S (Publicity)* [2003] HRLR 911 and the Supplement to para 4.52 above. **10.18**

n48 There may be a difference whether the breach of confidence relied on is a personal confidence or a trade secret: see the Supplement to para 9.35 above.

n54 See *Douglas v Hello! Ltd* [2003] 3 All ER 996 where Lindsay J at [229] stated that Parliament needed to step in to create a new free-standing tort of privacy insofar as any rights were not already protected by the fusion of the pre-existing law of confidence and the rights and duties created under the Human Rights Act 1998.

n55 In *Campbell v MGN Ltd*, the Court of Appeal held that the media exemption in s 32 of the Data Protection Act 1998 applied not only to the period before publication, but is of general application. See the Supplement to para 5.80 above.

n61 See now also the judgment of the Court of Appeal in *Campbell v Frisbee* [2003] EMLR 76 and the Supplement to paras 6.108–6.109 above.

(ii) *The rule against prior restraint*

See the Supplement to paras 7.35–7.52 above. **10.19–10.24**

See *Maccaba v Lichtenstein* [2002] EWHC 1325 (QB) where Morland J refused an application for an injunction to restrain an alleged threatened contempt of court on the basis that it was essentially a defamation action. **10.20**

(v) The argument against prior restraint in privacy

10.24   n84 In *Campbell v MGN Ltd*, the Court of Appeal held that the media exemption in s 32 of the Data Protection Act 1998 applied not only to the period before publication, but is of general application. See the Supplement to para 5.80 above.

(vi) Sufficient threat

10.25   n90 Two cases where an application has failed on this basis are *D v L* [2003] EWCA 1169 per Waller LJ at [28–29] (insufficient threat) and *Re S (Publicity)* [2003] HRLR 911 [77] and [112] (insufficient risk of further harm).

(b)   Preliminary procedural matters

(i)   The injunction should be drafted in clear and precise terms

10.26   n93 In *Douglas v Hello! Ltd* Lindsay J considered it odd that there should have been a difficulty in framing the injunction: [2003] 3 All ER 996 [223].

(iv) The hearing: private or public?

10.29   n102 The reference to the Civil Procedure Rules in this note should be to CPR r 39.2(4) not CPR r 29.3(2).

(c)   The jurisdiction of the Court and the principles to be applied

(i)   The Court's jurisdiction

10.30   In *D v L* [2003] EWCA 1169 [30] it appears that the Court would have exercised its discretion to refuse the injunction sought by reason of the behaviour of the applicant in sending offensive messages to the defendant, her advisers, and the judge.

(ii) The appropriate threshold test to be applied—American Cyanamid?

10.32–10.38   In *Cream Holdings Ltd v Banerjee* [2003] 2 All ER 318, the Court of Appeal felt it necessary finally to tackle head-on the question of precisely what test is meant to be applied under s 12(3) of the Act. The Court reached the conclusion that the test was not that of the balance of probabilities (as the words of the statute might on their face suggest) but rather that of a real prospect of success. The individual members of the Court of Appeal appear to have reached this conclusion by different routes. Simon Brown LJ made it clear at [61] that this (lower) threshold test 'merely gives the court a discretion in a greater number of cases. Often the court will not think it right to exercise that discretion in favour of prior restraint unless it is indeed satisfied that the claim will more probably than not succeed at trial.' Sedley LJ disagreed at [85] with Simon Brown LJ on this point, since it appeared to him to run the risk of some double-counting. See further the Supplement to paras 7.35–7.52 above and 10.64 below.

For an example of insufficient harm see *Re S (Publicity)* [2003] HRLR 911 [77].   **10.36**

(iii) Balance of convenience

Damages not adequate remedy.   In *Douglas v Hello! Ltd* [2003] 3 All ER 996   **10.43**
[271] Lindsay J viewed the matter from a different perspective. He indicated that
had the case for an interim injunction been presented primarily as one akin to a trade
secret it might have been successfully urged that by refusing an injunction because
damages sufficed the Court of Appeal would in effect be allowing a compulsory purchase by *Hello!* of a right to breach exclusiveness for which its trade rival had paid so
much and to do so despite the Court regarding the claimants as having sound claims
in confidence. Lindsay J referred to *Francome v Mirror Group Newspapers* [1984] 1
WLR 892 at 897 *per* Sir John Donaldson MR ('the right to disobey the law is not
obtainable by the payment of a penalty or licence fee').

(iv) Section 12(4): the importance of freedom of expression
See the Supplement to para 10.64 below.   **10.45–10.48**

(v) Section 12(4): Public domain, public interest, and relevant privacy codes

Public domain.   The limitation of the public domain defence in respect of per-   **10.50**
sonal information is especially relevant to photographs. In *Douglas v Hello! Ltd*
[2003] 3 All ER 996 [213]–[217], [278] Lindsay J held that the fact the
Douglases were about to, or to a limited extent had already, published their own
photographs thus putting 'information' into the public domain was no answer to
their claim against the unauthorised photographers and granted them a permanent injunction at trial, notwithstanding that the application for an interim injunction had failed. This approach was approved by Waller LJ in *D v L* [2003]
EWCA 1169 at [22].

About to become available to the public.   In *Douglas v Hello! Ltd* Lindsay J re-   **10.52**
garded the case of Lady Thatcher's memoirs as no longer binding: [2003] 3 All ER
996 [224]. See the Supplement to para 6.97 above.

Privacy codes.   See also *Douglas v Hello! Ltd* [2003] 3 All ER 996 at [204]–[205]   **10.53**
and the Supplement to para 9.07 n 12 above.

(vi) Balancing the right to privacy with the right to freedom of expression
In *Campbell v MGN Ltd* the Court of Appeal took the opportunity to correct   **10.61**
some of the common misunderstandings which had arisen from the comments of
Lord Woolf in *A v B plc* about the defence of public interest and the importance
of 'role models'. At [40]–[41] the Master of the Rolls stated that 'when Lord
Woolf spoke of the public having "an understandable and so a legitimate interest
in being told" information, even including trivial facts, about a public figure, he
was not speaking of private facts which a fair-minded person would consider it of-

fensive to disclose . . . For our part we would observe that the fact that an individual has achieved prominence on the public stage does not mean that his private life can be laid bare by the media. We do not see why it should necessarily be in the public interest that an individual who has been adopted as a role model, without seeking this distinction, should be demonstrated to have feet of clay.' In *Lady Archer v Williams* [2003] FSR 869, Jackson J took a restrictive view of the term 'role model', commenting at [64] that the claimant (the well-known wife of disgraced Tory peer and writer, Lord Archer) had been 'brought . . . under the spotlight of media attention . . . by the fact that she is married to Lord Archer and the nature of Lord Archer's various achievements and activities'. He did not regard her as being 'in the same category as the football player in *A v B plc*. Her professional and other activities do not make her private life a matter of legitimate interest to the public.' The importance of not elevating anyone in the public eye to the status of a role model was highlighted by Eady J in an address given at a seminar on privacy and the media, Gray's Inn, 12 December 2002.

10.63   The approach of Sedley LJ in *London Regional Transport Ltd v The Mayor of London* was adopted by Gray J in balancing the competing rights of confidentiality in documents held by the Jockey Club and the public interest in disclosing alleged wrongdoing in the racing world on an application by the BBC in the case of *Jockey Club v Buffham* [2002] QB 462.

10.64   In *Re S (Publicity)* [2003] HRLR 911 (a case on publicity concerning the child of a defendant in a criminal case, in which the Court's care jurisdiction was invoked on behalf of the child) the Court of Appeal held at [55]–[57] and [65] that where the courts have to strike a fair balance between the rights of the individual under Article 8 and the rights of the press under Article 10 in considering whether or not to make an order restraining a publication, the Court has to identify the extent to which refusing to grant the injunction would be a proportionate interference with the private life of the child and the extent to which granting it would be a proportionate interference with the right of the press to freedom of expression. In striking that balance, the Court of Appeal said that it had to bear in mind the effect that publicity will have on the child and the extent to which it will affect the ability of the Court to carry out its obligations to the child in the exercise of its care jurisdiction on the one hand, and, on the other, the effect that the order will have on the ability of the press to provide the public with a full and fair report of the proceedings bearing in mind the interest which the public has in knowing the identity of a defendant, which is one of the important and usually inevitable consequences of a public trial. See further the Supplement to para 4.52 above. It appears that the Court of Appeal in *Re S (Publicity)* considered that the test was similar in principle whether the jurisdiction invoked was the care jurisdiction, or an action in confidence: see [48] and the Supplement to para 4.89 above.

n174 See also *Douglas v Hello Ltd!* [2003] 3 All ER 996 at [186]–[187] where **10.65**
Lindsay J set out a similar list of principles to the *A v B plc* guidelines.

n176 In *Cumpana and Mazare v Romania*, Application no 33348/96, judgment
10 June 2003, [55] and *Lady Archer v Williams* [2003] FSR 869 [61] the courts
have had regard to the utility of the speech in question.

n177 See the Supplement to para 10.61 above.

n179 See also *D v L* [2003] EWCA 1169 at [18], paras 6.124–6.129 of the Main
Work and the Supplement to paras 9.35 and 10.43 above.

(3) Final or Perpetual Injunctions

(a) Final injunction as a remedy

See also *Jockey Club v Buffham* [2002] QB 462 and the Supplement to paras 6.136 **10.71**
and 10.50 above.

(b) Injunctions against the world (*contra mundum*)

The principle of granting an injunction against all the world was extended in '*X* **10.72**
a woman formerly known as Mary Bell and '*Y the daughter of X v News Group
Newspapers and MGN Ltd* [2003] FSR 850 at [63]–[64]. This practice was commented upon with approval by Lord Phillips MR in *Re S (Publicity)* [2003] HRLR
911 [98]–[99]. See the Supplement to para 6.136 above.

D. Damages

(1) The Availability of Damages in Principle

n201 The judge was overturned by the Court of Appeal on liability in *Campbell v* **10.76**
MGN Ltd but the availability of damages in principle was not questioned.
Damages were awarded for breach of confidence in *Lady Archer v Williams* [2003]
FSR 869 and in *Douglas v Hello! Ltd* [2003] EWHC 2629 (Ch). See the
Supplement to para 10.107 below.

(2) Discretionary or as of Right?

As to whether breach of privacy should be seen as a tort see the Supplement to para **10.78**
4.49 above.

n205 In *Campbell v MGN Ltd* the order was set aside by the Court of Appeal on
liability without comment on the size of the awards of damages.

n206 In *Douglas v Hello! Ltd* [2003] EWHC 2629, [59] Lindsay J stated he did
not regard the overall award made against the defendant, given its resources, 'as of
a size that is likely materially to stifle free expression'.

10.79 n207 The European Court found in *Peck v UK* (2003) 36 EHRR 41 that the applicant had suffered significant distress, embarrassment, and frustration which would not be sufficiently compensated by a finding of violation. The applicant was awarded 11,800 Euros in respect of non-pecuniary damage.

10.80 In *Anufrijeva v London Borough of Southwark* [2003] EWCA Civ 1406 [49]–[78] the Court of Appeal considered the features of claims for compensation under the HRA. In considering whether to award damages, and if so how much, a balance is to be drawn between the interests of the individual and those of the public as a whole. Damages are not an automatic entitlement but a remedy of last resort. Where no pecuniary loss is involved the court should consider whether other remedies granted to the successful complainant are sufficient to vindicate the right that has been infringed, taking into account the complainant's own responsibility for what has occurred. The approach is an equitable one and the scale and manner of the violation can be taken into account. In some cases distress or other non-pecuniary damage may be insufficient to require an award of compensation. The discretionary exercise of deciding whether to award compensation under the HRA is not to be compared with the approach adopted where damages are claimed for breach of an obligation under civil law, although the guidelines from the Judicial Studies Board, the Criminal Injuries Compensation Board and Parliamentary and Local Government Ombudsmen may assist. The Court also laid down guidelines as to the procedure for claims under s 8, HRA based on maladministration by a public body.

(3) Pecuniary Loss

10.82 n210 In *Irvine v Talksport* [2003] 2 All ER 881 [104], [106], [111] the Court of Appeal held that the principles identified by Lord Wilberforce in the *General Tire* case are applicable to the issue as to what would be a reasonable fee for the celebrity claimant's endorsement of the defendant's Talk Radio. A reasonable endorsement fee in the context of that case represented the fee which, on a balance of probabilities, the defendant would have had to pay in order to obtain lawfully that which it in fact obtained unlawfully, not the fee which the defendant could have afforded to pay. That was ascertained from the evidence of what the claimant said he would have accepted for endorsing the defendant, and from evidence of what he had accepted for other endorsements.

10.83 In *Douglas v Hello! Ltd* [2003] EWHC 2629 the personal claimants were awarded a sum in respect of additional costs caused to them by attempts to mitigate the effects of the breach of confidence.

10.87 See the Supplement to para 10.82 n 210 above.

10.90 In *Douglas v Hello! Ltd* [2003] EWHC 2629 it having been held that the defendants were liable to the corporate claimant in breach of confidence, the major battleground was the claim by OK! for loss of revenue caused by the publication of the unauthorised photographs. The court added the profit which OK! would have made but for the breach (with a reduction for losses too remote) to costs caused by attempted mitigation, arriving at a figure in excess of £1 million.

n224 In *Douglas v Hello! Ltd* [2003] EWHC 2629 Lindsay J did not decide as a matter of law whether a claim for damages on the basis of a notional licence fee was available because the mutually exclusive claim for compensatory damages yielded a higher figure in any event.

See the Supplement to para 10.82 n210 above.

In *Douglas v Hello! Ltd* [2003] EWHC 2629 [13] the claimants' claims for purely **10.91** compensatory damages (including pecuniary and non-pecuniary elements) and for a notional licence fee were held to be mutually exclusive; Lindsay J finding that a claimant could not properly claim for loss caused by something which he is to be taken to have notionally authorised. The claimants were permitted to run alternative claims on the basis that the court would make an award on whichever basis yielded the higher amount (with a warning of the costs consequences of so doing).

In *Anufrijeva v London Borough of Southwark* [2003] EWCA Civ 1406 the Court **10.92** of Appeal indicated that the approach to awarding damages under s 8, HRA should be no less liberal than that of the European Court of Human Rights.

(4) Non-pecuniary Loss

n233 The extent and consequences of the concession in *Campbell v MGN Ltd* **10.95** that no claim was made for infringement of privacy as such were explored by the Court of Appeal at [29]–[34].

In *Cumpana and Mazare v Romania,* Application no 33348/96, judgment of 10 **10.97** June 2003 (see the Supplement to para 2.13 above), the ECtHR held that reputation and honour are equally protected by Article 8 and Article 10(2) of the Convention. In that case the allegations were false in part, and the case came to the Court on the application of the publishers complaining of a breach of Article 10. It would appear to follow that damages for loss of reputation would be available under Article 8 for the unauthorised publication of private facts, whether true or false, in an appropriate case.

The defendant's appeal on liability was successful in *Campbell v MGN Ltd* as a re- **10.98** sult of which the damages were set aside.

The assumption that damages are available in principle for mental injury caused **10.100** by breach of confidence was not challenged by the Court of Appeal.

In *Douglas v Hello! Ltd* [2003] EWHC 2629 [57] a distinction was drawn between **10.101** distress caused by the knowledge that an intruder had been at the wedding (which was not attributable to Hello!) and the publication of the unauthorised photographs (which was).

(5) Quantum of Non-pecuniary Damages

10.107 The defendant's appeal on liability was successful in *Campbell v MGN Ltd* as a result of which the damages were set aside.

In *Lady Archer v Williams* [2003] FSR 869 the claimant sought damages for the disclosure in breach of confidence of the fact that she had undergone a facelift operation. Her primary claim was for the continuation of an injunction to restrain future breaches of confidence by her former personal assistant and she had stated expressly in evidence that the claim for damages was the least important part of her claim. On the basis of *Cornelius* and *Campbell* Jackson J accepted that where a breach of confidence causes injury to feelings the Court has the power to award damages. He said that general damages for injury to feelings should be kept to a modest level, should be proportionate to the injury suffered, and should be well below the level of general damages for serious physical or psychiatric injury. He assessed general damages at £2,500.

In *Douglas v Hello! Ltd* [2003] EWHC 2629 [57] the personal claimants were awarded £3,750 each for the distress caused by publication of the unauthorised photographs.

10.108 The Radio 1 DJ Sara Cox received a settlement of £50,000 from *The People* newspaper and a photographer in June 2003 over the publication of pictures of her and her husband naked on their honeymoon. It is notable that following the intervention of the PCC *The People* had already published a 63-word apology at the top of page three in the issue immediately following the publication complained of.

(6) Aggravated Damages

10.110 On appeal in *Campbell v MGN Ltd* the defendant argued that an award of aggravated damages in this context needed to be supported by a finding that the opinions expressed by the defendant's journalists were not honestly held. However the Court of Appeal (necessarily *obiter* because of the finding on liability) said at [139] that the terms of the articles relied on by the claimant justified the findings made by the judge and that it would have been open to him to award aggravated damages had his findings on liability been valid. In *Douglas v Hello! Ltd* [2003] 3 All ER 996 Lindsay J was invited to award aggravated damages. He assumed that an award of aggravated damages was available but held the behaviour of *Hello!* not to be high-handed or oppressive or so flagrant or offensive as to justify an award of aggravated damages.

(7) Exemplary Damages

In *Anufrijeva v London Borough of Southwark* [2003] EWCA Civ 1406 the Court of Appeal stated that exemplary damages were not available under s 8, HRA. **10.116**

In *Douglas v Hello! Ltd* [2003] EMLR 601 Morritt V-C permitted the pleading of a claim for exemplary damages. At trial the claim failed: *Douglas v Hello! Ltd* [2003] 3 All ER 996 [272]–[273]. Lindsay J drew three principles from *Kuddus* namely (1) the question of whether to award exemplary damages should be determined by reference to the nature of the behaviour complained of rather than by reference to the specific cause of action; (2) a powerful case can be made that such damages should be considered where 'and perhaps only where' the behaviour complained of gives rise to a sense of outrage; and (3) a recognised category in which such damages may be awarded is where damages on an ordinary compensatory basis can be seen not to be sufficient to do justice. He was content to assume, without deciding, that exemplary damages 'or equity's equivalent' were available in breach of confidence. There was no need to decide the point because he held that the other two limbs of the test were not satisfied. He held that to describe the conduct of *Hello!* as outrageous would be to overstate the matter, particularly in an industry in which 'intrusion into privacy and little regard for each other's business rights have . . . been not unknown' and that he was not satisfied that equitable compensation would yield a figure such that *Hello!*'s profit would exceed the compensation due to the claimants, nor that *Hello!* had ever calculated that it might do so. On making the total award of £1,047,756 Lindsay J stated that although this substantial figure did not go beyond the compensatory into the penal it was such 'as may make *Hello!* alive to the unwisdom of acting as it did': [2003] EWHC 2629 [59]. **10.119**

(8) Mitigation of Damage

The Court of Appeal in *Douglas v Hello! Ltd* recited the trial judge's finding at [28] and added at [41]: 'For our part we would observe that the fact that an individual has achieved prominence on the public stage does not mean that his private life can be laid bare by the media. We do not see why it should necessarily be in the public interest that an individual who has been adopted as a role model, without seeking this distinction, should be demonstrated to have feet of clay.' This formula suggests that those public figures who have sought to make themselves role models are entitled to less damages for an unjustified invasion of privacy than those who have not. **10.121**

11

FREEDOM OF INFORMATION AND NEWSGATHERING

A. Introduction

An injunction may be granted to prohibit the publication of images or sound **11.02** recordings of conversations which are made improperly, whether or not the information is in the public domain, and whether or not there are reasons why the information in it may be published by other means: *D v L* [2003] EWCA 1169, [23], [24] (tape recording taken by one person of a private conversation with another without the consent of that other). Examples of occasions when it may be in the public interest to permit use of surreptitiously obtained images or recordings are given at [27], eg to provide proof that the public are being misled. The state may also be liable for the publication in the media of documents leaked from official records: *Craxi (No 2) v Italy*, Application no 25337/94, judgment of 17 July 2003, [72]–[76] and see the Supplement to paras 6.40 and 12.25 and 12.31 below.

n3 Even where use is permitted in court of information obtained by unlawful means, the Court may seek to deter improper conduct, and reflect its disapproval, by means of a costs order: *Jones v Warwick University* [2003] 1 WLR 954. See further the Supplement to para 9.47 above.

B. Obtaining Information from Public Authorities

11.04 The rolling programme of implementation of the Freedom of Information Act 2000 began on schedule in November 2002 and is still due to be completed by January 2005.

(4) Freedom of Information Act 2000

(b) Code of Practice for public authorities acting under the FOIA

11.16 The position set out in this paragraph has been altered as follows. Initially the Lord Chancellor took over the Secretary of State's responsibilities under s 45, FOIA. He issued the *Lord Chancellor's Code of Practice on the discharge of public authorities' functions under Part I of the FOIA* in November 2002. Part VII of this Code sets out the relevant guidelines regarding the requirement to consult with third parties. Paragraph 31 refers to the relevant legal rights of third parties as being, by way of example, those relating to the common law duty of confidence and where the relevant information constitutes 'personal data' those within the DPA. Paras 36–38 deal with situations where consultation is not or may not be appropriate. The Lord Chancellor's responsibilities in this and other respects have now been transferred to the newly created Secretary of State for Constitutional Affairs (Secretary of State for Constitutional Affairs Order 2003 (SI 2003/1887)).

(c) Information obtained from entities other than public authorities

11.17 As a result of the decision in *R (Robertson) v City of Wakefield Metropolitan Council* an amendment was made to the Representation of the People Act (England and Wales) Regulations 2001 by the Representation of the People (England and Wales) (Amendment) Regulations 2002. It provides that the Electoral Registration Officers shall maintain two registers—the full register, available to all for inspection and available for sale to credit reference agencies for credit control purposes and the control of fraud, and the edited register, which excludes those who requested to be excluded, and is available for sale without restriction. A challenge to the new regulations in *R (Robertson) v Home Secretary* [2003] EWHC 1760 Admin failed. It was held that the sale of the full register to commercial concerns in the specified circumstances struck a permissible balance between the public interest in the facilitation of credit and the control of fraud and the right to vote. For further discussion of privacy and addresses see the Supplement to para 6.54 above.

n28 The first decision in *Robertson* is now reported at [2002] QB 1052.

(5) The Identification of Victims of Crime and Accidents Under the Data Protection Act 1998

n33 Note that the current Information Commissioner is Mr Richard Thomas. **11.19** The Guidance Notes referred in this paragraph, which are part of the series of Media Advisory Group Guidelines produced by ACPO, can be found on its website at http://www.acpo.police.uk under 'Policies'.

C. Media Codes of Practice and Related Legislation

(1) Codes of Practice

Note that under the Communications Act 2003, which received the Royal Assent **11.22** on 17 July 2003, the functions of the five regulatory bodies, the BSC, the ITC, the Radio Authority, Oftel, and the Radiocommunications Agency, have been merged into the Office of Communications (Ofcom) which became operational at the end of 2003. See further the Supplement to para 4.31 above.

(2) Human Rights Act 1998

See the approach of Lindsay J in *Douglas v Hello! Ltd* [2003] 3 All ER 996 **11.27** [186(vi)–(viii)], [204]–[205], and the Supplement to para 9.07 above.

n47 *A v B plc* is now reported at [2003] QB 195. **11.28**

It is now established that the improper means by which information is obtained may provide a basis for a claim in confidence independently of any relationship between the parties: see the Supplement to para 11.03 above, and paras 6.124–6.129 of the Main Work.

(3) Data Protection Act 1998

In *Campbell v MGN Ltd* [2003] QB 633 the Court held at [128] that the media **11.29** exemption in s 32 applies not only to the period before publication, but is of general application: see further the Supplement to paras 5.05, 5.32, and 5.80 above.

The fact that a newspaper may have published information about an individual before the DPA 1998 came into force does not mean that a subsequent publication is exempted under the transitional provisions in Sch 8 para 1(1) of the Act: *Douglas v Hello! Ltd* [2003] 3 All ER 996 [233]–[235].

(a) Disclosure of the purpose

In *Douglas v Hello! Ltd* [2003] 3 All ER 996 [236] Lindsay J held that the **11.30** surreptitious circumstances in which the photographs had been obtained in that case pointed to the processing (in particular the publication) as having not been fair.

(b) Procuring illegal disclosure

11.33   n60 *Ashworth Hospital Authority v MGN Ltd* is now reported at [2002] 1 WLR 2033.

n62 Contrast the Court of Appeal decision in *Cream Holdings v Banerjee* [2003] EMLR 323—where the Court of Appeal upheld an interim injunction to restrain the publication of details of alleged financial irregularities disclosed to newspapers in breach of confidence—with the decision of Gray J in *Jockey Club v Buffham* [2003] QB 462, where the Court refused to restrain the BBC from publishing details of an alleged horseracing scandal, partly on grounds of public interest.

D. Trespass, Nuisance, Harassment, and Distress

(1) Trespass

11.35   In *Grosse v Purvis* [2003] QDC 151 [459]–[462], [486]–[489] a Queensland court awarded very substantial damages for trespass to land against a stalker, as well as damages for a claim in privacy. Skoien J said: 'There is no evidence of any real damage (in dollar terms) other than emotional upset and annoyance to the plaintiff. In my view compensatory damages for trespass should be assessed at $25,000 ($20,000 to date). This includes vindicatory damages. However, the persistent, offensive and defiant nature of the trespass calls for a substantial increase in that award by a further sum of $25,000 for aggravated damages ($20,000 to date) making a total of $50,000.'

(2) Nuisance

11.46   In *Grosse v Purvis* [2003] QDC 151 [463]–[465], in addition to a claim in privacy, a claim in nuisance was upheld in respect of events 'where the evidence does not establish actual entry on the plaintiff's premises but conduct of the defendant elsewhere which affected her enjoyment of her premises'. Skoien J said at [490]: 'This cause of action is made out and the damage is of greater moment than for the trespass because it includes the trespass. I assess compensatory damages at $30,000 ($20,000 to date), this sum to include vindicatory damages and aggravated damages at $30,000 ($20,000 to date), a total of $60,000.' *Hunter v Canary Wharf* was not cited in the judgment.

(3) Harassment

11.49   In *Grosse v Purvis* [2003] QDC 151 [417], [448]–[451], a claim in harassment was held to be synonymous with the claim in privacy which was upheld. There is a harassment statute in Queensland, Criminal Code s 359E, but the statute does not itself confer a right to make a claim for damages. See further the Supplement to para 2.64 above.

(4) Distress

In *Grosse v Purvis* [2003] QDC 151 [452]–[455] the Queensland court upheld, amongst other claims against a stalker, a claim for intentional infliction of harm (*Wilkinson v Downton*). It was accepted that mere distress was not sufficient to make out the cause of action. There had to be damage in the form of an injury to mental health that is capable of causing a recognisable physical condition, or to put it another way, a psychiatric illness. The post-traumatic stress disorder the plaintiff suffered from in that case represented such physical harm.   **11.60**

The correctness of the observations of McGechan J in *Tucker* has however been doubted by Randerson J in the much more recent case of *Hosking v Runting* (High Court of New Zealand, 30 May 2003), which contains a detailed analysis of the development of privacy laws in the UK, Australia, and the USA. See further the Supplement to paras 2.63 and 4.12–4.14 above.   **11.61**

n118 The House of Lords upheld the Court of Appeal's ruling in *Wainwright v Home Office* that there should be no liability under *Wilkinson v Downton* for distress which does not amount to recognised psychiatric injury and so far as there may be a tort of intention under which such damage is recoverable, the necessary intention was not established on the facts of the case: [2003] 3 WLR 1137 [47]. See the Supplement to paras 4.83–4.88 above.   **11.62**

None of the comparative jurisprudence cited in argument in *Wainwright v Home Office* is referred to in their Lordships' judgments, but on the extent to which English law recognises a general right to privacy the House clearly preferred the approach of the High Court of New Zealand in *Hosking v Runting* to that of the Queensland District Court in *Grosse v Purvis*. Thus it would appear, ironically, that some Commonwealth jurisdictions may have founded a cause of action in privacy based, at least in part, on the perceived development of English common law (*Douglas v Hello! Ltd* is cited in support of this development in *Grosse v Purvis* at [434]) whereas English law, as declared by the House of Lords, does not in fact recognise such a right. See further the Supplement to paras 1.01, 2.64, 3.03, and 4.05 n 7 above.

12

PRIVACY AND THE ADMINISTRATION OF JUSTICE

A. Introduction

(1) The Overriding Principle

(c) Article 6(1) of the Convention

12.06   See now *Re S (Publicity)* [2003] HRLR 911 [44], [86], and para 4.52 above.

C. Control of Access to Court Documents

12.25   In *Craxi (No 2) v Italy*, Application no 25337/94, judgment of 17 July 2003, [73] and [76], it was held that where records of intercepted telephone calls (ie those which were not relevant to the proceedings, and so not read out in court) were leaked to the press from the Court Registry there was a breach by the State of its obligation to secure the right to respect for private life and correspondence. It was further held that in the case of such a leak it is the obligation of the State to carry out effective inquiries to rectify the matter to the extent possible: [74]–[75]. For proceedings brought on a similar basis in respect of documents leaked from a Ministry see *Lord Ashcroft v (1) Attorney-General and (2) Department For International Development* [2002] EWHC 1122 (QB).

(5) Power of the Parties to Waive Privacy and Disseminate Documents on the Court File

12.31   In criminal proceedings it has been held that the State has a positive obligation to edit or redact the contents of intercepted telephone communications made by the accused so that those which have little or no connection with the criminal charges are not read out in open court: *Craxi (No 2) v Italy*, Application no 25337/94, judgment of 17 July 2003, [66]. Where the prosecution proposes to use such material it must provide the accused and the judge with an opportunity to exclude those communications which do not avail the parties to the proceedings and could adversely and uselessly interfere with the accused person's right to respect for private life and correspondence: [80]. Where this procedure was not adopted, the reading out of such material was not in accordance with law: [82]–[84]. The same principle would appear to apply to all communications protected by Article 8. It remains to be determined what are the positive obligations of the Court in proceedings to which a public authority is not a party. It would appear that any consequential publication of such material in the press will amount to a breach by the State of its obligations under Article 8: [57], [66]–[73].

E. Restrictions on the Reporting of Proceedings Held in Public

(1) Restrictions on Reporting Hearings in Open Court

n92 The passage cited from the judgment of Buxton LJ in *Lilly Icos v Pfizer Ltd* **12.57**
(No 2) [2002] 1 All ER 842 is at 851, not at 284 as incorrectly stated in the Main
Work. The case is also reported in [2002] IP & T 274, where the relevant passage
is at 284, and in [2002] 1 WLR 2253, where the relevant passage is at 2261.

There may be a positive obligation upon the Court to restrict reporting of information which is protected by Article 8, but which is read out in court in spite of
the fact that it is irrelevant to the proceedings: *Craxi (No 2) v Italy*, Application
no 25337/94, judgment of 17 July 2003: see the Supplement to para 12.31
above.

(2) Privacy Protection for Adults Before the Human Rights Act 1998

In *R v Felixstowe JJ, ex p Leigh* [1987] 1 All ER 551, 561d it was held that the pub- **12.58**
lic are entitled to know names, but not addresses, of justices. See *R (Al-Pawwaz) v
Brixton Prison Governor* [2002] 2 WLR 101, [82]–[86] for the limited circumstances in which the identification of witnesses can be withheld.

*(3) Privacy Protection for Adults After the Coming into Force of the Human
Rights Act 1998*

See *Craxi (No 2) v Italy*, Application no 25337/94, judgment of 17 July 2003 and **12.62–12.68**
the Supplement to paras 12.31 and 12.57 above. Where the admission of video
recording was held likely to infringe the Article 8 rights of a third party (a child depicted incidentally) and possibly of the adult parties to the litigation, the
Employment Appeal Tribunal has held that it is obliged under the equivalent provision of its own rules (The Employment Tribunal Rules of Procedure 2001, rule
10(3)), to view the recordings in private: XXX v (1) YYY (2) ZZZ), EAT, 9 April
2003, at [23].

(4) Children

(a) Privacy protection for children before the Human Rights Act 1998

See the Supplement to para 4.52 above and *Re S (Publicity)* [2003] HRLR 911. **12.72**

(d) Privacy protection for children after the Human Rights Act 1998

See the Supplement to paras 4.52, 12.62–12.68 above and *Re S (Publicity)* [2003] **12.84**
HRLR 911.

F. Restrictions on the Use of Material that is Disclosed in the Course of Court Proceedings

(6) Limit and Extent of the Duty of Confidence

12.102   The Court's observation in the *Prudential* case holds true for the CPR regime. The imposition under CPR r 31.22(1) of an express obligation on the receiving party not to make collateral use of disclosed documents subsumes any private law duty of confidence which might otherwise be owed by the receiving party to the disclosing party or to a third party. The further use of documents disclosed under the CPR regime is governed by sub-paragraphs (a)–(c) of CPR r 31.22(1) and CPR r 31.22(2), and not by any private law rights. However it is implicit from the approach of the Court of Appeal in *Lilly Icos v Pfizer Ltd (No 2)* that a court can take account of relevant private law rights when considering an application under CPR r 31.22(3) for an order restricting or prohibiting the use of a disclosed document that has been referred to in open court. See the Supplement to para 12.111 below.

(7) Release of the Implied Undertaking

(b) The privacy right overrides the reporting right

12.111   It is to be noted that under CPR r 31.22(2) the Court can make an order restricting or prohibiting the use of a document which has been disclosed, even where the document has been read to or by the court, or referred to, at a hearing held in public. An application for such an order may be made by a party or by any person to whom the document belongs. It follows that under the CPR regime not only does the privacy right override the reporting right where the disclosed document is only referred to in a private hearing, but it may also prevail where the disclosed document is referred to in a public hearing. Whether the privacy right will prevail in such circumstances is likely to depend in part upon the extent to which the contents of the document have received publicity during the hearing. In *Lilly Icos v Pfizer (No 2)* the Court of Appeal decided to make an order prohibiting the use of a patentee's schedule of advertising figures on the grounds that the schedule was commercially confidential and it had only been referred to in passing during the public hearing, and not as part of any argumentative submissions. See further para 6.64 n181 and paras 6.89–6.91 of the Main Work and the Supplement to paras 12.31 and 12.57 above.

13

THE PRIVACY CODES

A. Introduction

The Communications Act 2003 received Royal Assent in July 2003, and Ofcom **13.01** began to fulfil its duties in December 2003. The body has indicated that part of its remit will be to look afresh at the codes of each of the existing regulatory bodies, and it may write a completely new, codified set of 'rules'. While Ofcom will replace the Radio Authority, the Broadcasting Standards Commission, and the Independent Television Commission, the BBC will also be accountable to the body on issues of taste and decency.

13.02 In *Peck v UK* (2003) 36 EHRR 41 the Court found that the lack of legal power of the self-regulatory commissions to award damages to a complainant meant that those bodies could not provide an effective remedy to him, within the meaning of Article 13 ECHR. The Court noted that the ITC's power to impose a fine on the relevant television company did not amount to an award of damages to Mr Peck. The Court also noted that neither the BSC not the PCC had the power to prevent publications or broadcasts.

B. The Human Rights Act 1998

13.08 See, eg Lindsay J's consideration of the PCC's Code when considering s 12, HRA in *Douglas v Hello! Ltd* [2003] 3 All ER 996 [205].

(1) What is a 'Relevant Privacy Code'?

13.09 In *Campbell v Frisbee* [2002] EMLR 31, an action for breach of confidence, the judge at first instance held that the code of practice of the PCC was not a relevant privacy code in the circumstances of the case. Although section 12(4) HRA itself was relevant as the information provided to the *News of the World* by Miss Campbell's former assistant, Miss Frisbee, constituted 'journalistic material', Lightman J considered that the Code had no application to Miss Frisbee and did not lay down standards in respect of compliance or otherwise with obligations of confidence on her part. On appeal, the defendant contended that there was good reason to treat a newspaper and its source of information on the same basis in that it is often only through informants that the media obtain stories in which the public have a legitimate interest: the legitimacy of the publication of a story under the Code was relevant when considering the legitimacy of the act of the informant in providing the story to the media. Whilst the Court of Appeal did not need to decide this issue, it held that the point was 'arguable': [2003] EMLR 3.

C. The Data Protection Act 1998

13.13 In fact, the exemption applies to the processing of any material either before or after publication, and to the publication itself (*Campbell v MGN Ltd* [2003] QB 633).

13.15 Proper compliance with a relevant code of practice may assist a defendant in avoiding liability after publication in a data protection claim, as well as evading prior restraint, as the exemption applies before and after publication and to the publication itself (see the Supplement to para 5.80 above). Conversely, a lack of compliance will not necessarily mean that a defendant cannot avail himself of the s 32 exemption. In *Campbell*, the Court of Appeal held that MGN had satisfied the requirements for exemption under s 32 in publishing an article and accompanying photographs of Miss Campbell emerging from Narcotics Anonymous, notwith-standing that the judge at first instance had found that the covert photography of the claimant was 'contrary to the letter and spirit' of the PCC's Code: [135].

F. The Codes and Adjudications

(1) The Right to Privacy

Examples of material that has been considered 'private' by the PCC include infor-   **13.42**
mation concerning a complainant's rental payments (Mrs Kim Noble and *Jersey Evening Post*, 6 December 2001 (Report 57)), confidential information about a complainant's health (Mrs Judith Tonner and *News of the World*, 21 July 2002 (Report 60)), and personal correspondence (Mrs Primrose Shipman and *The Mirror*, 9 July 2001 (Report 56)).

(a) Who can complain?

The PCC does not consider that 'questions of privacy and intrusion' can relate to   **13.47**
a deceased person: Messrs Manches on behalf of the Tolkien family and *Sunday Mercury*, 26 January 2003 (Report 62). See further the Supplement to para 6.146 n 456 above.

(3) Public Figures

n72 The Court of Appeal in *Campbell v MGN Ltd* [40] qualified Lord Woolf's   **13.55**
comments in *A v B plc* [2002] 3 WLR 542 at [11(xii)] as follows:

> When Lord Woolf spoke of the public having 'an understandable and so a legiti-mate interest in being told information, even including trivial facts, about a public figure', he was not speaking of private facts which a fair-minded person would con-sider it offensive to disclose. That is clear from his subsequent commendation of the guidance on striking a balance between Article 8 and Article 10 rights provided by the Council of Europe Resolution 1165 of 1998.

The Court affirmed that one principle arising from the development of the law of confidentiality to accommodate Article 8 and Article 10 was that 'where a public figure chooses to make untrue pronouncements about his or her private life, the press will normally be entitled to put the record straight': [43].

(4) Information Already in the Public Domain

In a complaint brought by Suranne Jones, an actress in the television soap   **13.63**
Coronation Street, against the *Daily Sport*, the Court had to consider the extent to which the complainant had 'acquiesced' in stories about her private life:

Suranne Jones and *Daily Sport,* 22 May 2003 (Report 63). The article complained of featured explicit revelations by the complainant's former boyfriend about their relationship. The newspaper claimed in its defence that both it and the *News of the World* had published similar accounts from the same source three years previously without objection from the complainant. The Commission said it had expressed the view that people should complain whenever material is published that they consider intrusive and that it would balance whether the extent of an individual's acquiescence in stories about their private life is sufficient to justify a newspaper publishing further intrusive material about them. In this case, the subject matter was of the most personal nature and graphically described and had no public interest. The complainant's failure to complain three years previously about a small number of interviews with the same ex-boyfriend was not sufficient reason to justify the publication of such an intrusive article.

13.63   See also Schillings Solicitors on behalf of Bernie Ecclestone and *The Mail on Sunday,* 25 August 2002 (Report 60).

13.64   See also Miss Julie Goodyear MBE and *The People,* 6 October 2002 (Report 61) where the PCC held that the complainant's previous willingness to negotiate contracts with *The People* for features and photographs of her home was not sufficient reason for the respondent's publication of long-lens photographs of her in her back garden where she had a 'reasonable expectation of privacy'.

(5) Disclosure of Private Address

13.73   See also Ms. Dynamite and *Islington Gazette,* 26 March 2003 (Report 63) where an article on the singer reported that she had purchased a new property in North London, and featured the name of the street and a photograph of the property. The Commission held that sufficient details were included in the article to identify the property and upheld the complainant's complaint under clause 3.

(6) Ordinary People in the News

(a) CCTV Recordings

13.78   See now *Peck v UK* (2003) 36 EHRR 41 and the Supplement to para 2.35 above.

(b) Individuals in times of grief or shock

13.79   See, eg Messrs Manches on behalf of the Tolkien family and *Sunday Mercury,* 26 January 2003 (Report 62) and A couple and *Esher News & Mail,* 12 June 2002 (Report 59).

13.81   See also *Back to the Floor:* BBC2, 27 November 2001 (Bulletin 56) in which the BSC found a breach of its Code where the victim of an accident refused consent to be filmed, but programme-makers filmed and broadcast footage of him receiving

medical attention nonetheless, and Tom Pontifex and *First Sight: On a Knife Edge*:
BBC2, 7 February 2002 (Bulletin 68).

(7) The Identification of Innocent People

n121 See *Slave Nation: Protest*: Channel 4, 22 August 2001 (Bulletin 50) where a   **13.87**
participant in a protest who knew she was being filmed but had made it clear to
programme-makers that she did not want to appear in the programme complained at her identification. The BSC found that the programme-makers should
have offered her the opportunity of having her identity concealed.

n 124 See also the BSC's adjudication in *ITV News at Ten*: Carlton, 16 January
2002 (Bulletin 54).

(10) Long-lens Photography and 'Private Places'

See also *Douglas v Hello! Ltd* [205] where Lindsay J held that, 'the very same prin-   **13.111**
ciple in the [PCC] Code that provides that the use of long lenses to take pictures
of people in private places without their consent was unacceptable must . . . inescapably also make the surreptitious use of short lenses to take pictures of people
in private places without their consent at least equally unacceptable'. The Court
held that, in the circumstances of that case, the PCC's Code was breached.

See *Campbell v MGN Ltd* [135], however, where the judge at first instance found   **13.115**
that covert photography of Naomi Campbell emerging from a Narcotics
Anonymous meeting, onto a public street, was 'contrary to the letter and spirit of the
[PCC] code'; this finding did not appear to be challenged by the Court of Appeal.

In Hugh Tunbridge and *Dorking Advertiser*, 23 May 2002, the PCC upheld a pri-   **13.118**
vacy complaint, considering that customers of a quiet café could expect to sit in-
side such an establishment without having to worry that surreptitious
photographs would be taken of them and published in newspapers (Report 58).

See *East Midlands Today*: BBC1, 6 December 2001 (Bulletin 60) in which the   **13.123**
BSC held that the filming of a school from outside the school's grounds did not
amount to an infringement of the school's privacy.

(11) Children

Consent must emanate from the child's legal guardian, and must be clear and un-   **13.126**
equivocal: Sally Everitt and Mr Andy Brick and *Welwyn & Hatfield Times*, 27
January 2003 (Report 61). See also Mr Colin Eves and *Brecon & Rednor Express*,
27 September 2001 (Report 57) where the PCC held that where a photograph of
a boy had been taken at school, it was the consent of the school which was relevant
and not that of his mother. The consent of a child is irrelevant: Mrs S Granton and
Daily Post, 3 August 2002 (Report 59).

13.127   The Commission's reasoning in complaints falling under clause 6 of the code is well illustrated in the complaint brought by the actress Kate Beckinsale against the *Daily Mail*, 15 April 2003 (Report 63). The article, entitled 'Mummy's latest love scene leaves Lily unimpressed', reported that the complainant was in a new relationship and included a series of pictures of her embracing and kissing her new partner. In one of the pictures, the complainant's daughter Lily was featured apparently ignoring her mother's romantic activity. In adjudicating the complaint under clause 6, the Commission asked itself whether Lily had been photographed in a private place. It concluded that she had not. It then asked itself whether the article contained material about the child's private life that was only published because of the fame of her mother. It held that the article contained no private details about Lily—such as her health, or schooling—but recorded general observations about her apparent reaction to her surroundings. Third, given that the photographs were published without consent, could publication have damaged Lily's welfare? The Commission noted that images of Lily had already been put into the public domain without complaint from her mother. In rejecting the complaint on this ground as well the Commission distinguished a previous ruling where 'photos of the daughter of a well-known individual appeared for the first time leading to her general identification'. It is presumed that the Commission is referring to the complaint brought by JK Rowling against *OK!* magazine considered at para 13.67 of the Main Work.

13.132   See, eg *Sleepers: Undercover with the Racists*: Channel 4, 29 November 2001, (Bulletin 63), where the BSC took the complainant's age into account when finding that the identification of him uttering a racist comment in secretly filmed footage was not in the overriding public interest (although the footage itself was).

G. The Regulatory Bodies as Public Authorities

(1) Are the Media Regulators 'Public Authorities' Under the Human Rights Act 1998?

13.135   n207 The reference in this note should be to *Hansard*, HL not HC.

13.136   The House of Lords disapproved of the Court of Appeal's reasoning in *Aston Cantlow and Wilmcote with Billesley Parochial Church Council v Wallbank* [2003] 3 WLR 283 and laid down their own criteria for assessing whether a body owed a duty to act compatibly with Convention rights under s 6 HRA. Their Lordships held that the concept of 'public authority' equated to bodies whose nature or functions were broadly governmental. Thus in the case of 'core' or 'standard' public authorities (such as government departments, local authorities, the police and armed forces which are required to act compatibly with Convention rights in everything they do) the relevant factors include the possession of special powers, democratic accountability, public funding in whole or in part, an obligation to act only in the public interest, and a statutory constitution: [7]. In the case of 'hybrid' or 'functional' public authorities (which have certain public functions but are not required to act compatibly with Convention rights in respect of acts which are private in nature) there is no single test of universal application. Factors to be taken into account include the extent to which in carrying out the relevant function the body is publicly funded, or is exercising statutory powers, or is taking the place of central government or local authorities, or is providing a public service: [12].

The Court of Appeal in *R (Beer) v Hampshire Farmers Markets Ltd* (2003) 31 EG 67, expressing surprise that there was no reference to *Poplar Housing Association Ltd v Donoghue* [2002] QB 48 or *R (Heather) v Leonard Cheshire Foundation* [2002] 2 All ER 936 by the House of Lords in *Aston Cantlow*, held that those two authorities would continue to be a source of valuable guidance as to what amounts to the exercise by a hybrid authority of functions of a public nature.

There is thus no reason to depart from the view expressed in this paragraph that the PCC is likely to be considered to be a hybrid public authority which, in the exercise of its adjudicatory functions, is under a duty to act compatibly with Convention rights under s 6 HRA.

It was confirmed in *Aston Cantlow* at [52] and *Beer* at [27]–[28] that it is possible **13.138** to conclude that a decision by a public authority is not amenable to judicial review and vice versa. The domestic case law on judicial review can be 'very helpful' but reliance on domestic cases must be tempered by, and sometime, yield to, relevant Strasbourg jurisprudence. That is because the scheme of the HRA is to replicate as far as possible the circumstances in which the United Kingdom's responsibility would be engaged before the ECtHR. Consequently, that jurisprudence is especially likely to be helpful in determining whether a body is a core public authority. It is likely to be less helpful in relation to the fact-sensitive question of whether in an individual case a hybrid body is exercising a public function.

n224 The explanation given in this note is now accepted as the rationale behind s 6 HRA. See the Supplement to para 1.81 n 218 above.

n229 The Court of Appeal's decision in *R (ProLife Alliance) v BBC* was reversed **13.141** by the House of Lords: [2003] 2 WLR 1403. Their Lordships showed a greater willingness than the Court of Appeal had done to defer to the broadcasters' assessment of what material was likely to be offensive to public feeling when they banned an anti-abortion election broadcast. The obligation not to broadcast offensive material is placed on the independent broadcasters by Parliament (under s 6(1)(a) Broadcasting Act 1990) and by the Government on the BBC (under para 5.1(d) of its agreement with the Secretary of State for National Heritage). The House held that the Court of Appeal had asked itself the wrong question and 'in effect carried out its own balancing exercise between the requirements of freedom of political speech and the protection of the public from being unduly distressed in their own homes' [16]. Since Article 10 in this context does not confer a right on everyone to express their own opinion on television, but a right to 'fair consideration for being afforded the opportunity to do so' [58] the real issue was 'whether the requirements of taste and decency are a discriminatory, arbitrary or unreasonable condition for allowing a political party free access at election time to a particular public medium' [62].

Lord Hoffmann preferred not to see the exercise of identifying the limits of a decision maker's powers as a matter of 'courtesy or deference' ('with its overtones of servility, or perhaps gracious concession') but as a question of law: [75]–[76]. It is submitted that that may be true as a matter of classification but it does not help to identify the relevant criteria needed to determine whether those limits have been exceeded. Such guidance as is given is not very helpful. As Lord Hoffmann said: 'once one accepts that the broadcasters were entitled to apply generally accepted standards [of what is offensive], I do not see how it is possible for a court to say that they were wrong. Public opinion in these matters is often diverse, sometimes unexpected and in constant flux. Generally accepted standards on these questions are not a matter of intuition on the part of elderly male judges': [79]–[80]. It would appear that nothing short of irrationality would have rendered the broadcasters' decision unlawful. The fact that the BBC conceded for the purposes of the case that it would be unlawful for it to act incompatibly with Convention rights under s 6 HRA would appear to have made no difference. Lord Hoffmann attached 'some importance' to the fact that two of the decision-makers were women. This, apparently, gave them greater expertise than the court to assess the likely effect of the broadcast on the 200,000 women in the UK who have abortions every year. On this reasoning, the decision of a body entrusted with decision-making powers is more likely to be respected by the court if it comprises of at least some members of the class of people most likely to be effected by its decision.

More useful guidance on the degree of latitude to be afforded to the decision-maker is contained in Laws LJ's dissenting judgment in *International Transport Roth GmbH v Secretary of State for the Home Department* [2002] 3 WLR 344, 376–8 which was cited with apparent approval by Lord Walker in *ProLife* at [136]:

—greater deference is to be paid to an Act of Parliament than to a decision of the executive or subordinate measure;
—there is more scope for deference where the Convention itself requires a balance to be struck, much less so where the right is stated in terms which are unqualified;
—greater deference will be due to the democratic powers where the subject-matter in hand is peculiarly within their constitutional responsibility, and less when it lies more particularly within the constitutional responsibility of the courts;

—greater or less deference will be due according to whether the subject matter lies within the actual or potential expertise of the democratic powers or the courts.

However, these principles still leave a great deal of uncertainty which can only be resolved on the facts of a particular case. Perhaps the most that can be said at this stage in the bedding-down process of the HRA is, as Lord Walker concludes at [139], that the court's task is 'to review the decision with an intensity appropriate to all the circumstances of the case.'

n230 The PCC was precluded from adjudicating in respect of a complaint from the DJ Sara Cox because the same matter was the subject of legal proceedings. See new para 1.62B above.   **13.142**

The European Court of Human Rights has now confirmed that the PCC and other media regulators are incapable of giving an effective remedy because they lack the powers to award damages or grant injunctions: *Peck v UK* (2003) 36 EHRR 41. See the Supplement to paras 1.69 and 13.02 above.   **13.143**

The European Court's decision in *Peck* would appear to encourage successful complainants to the media regulators to seek to 'top up' their favourable adjudications with an award of damages from the court. Both the BSC and ITC upheld Mr Peck's complaints of invasion of privacy under their respective codes and the European Court granted him an additional 11,800 Euros (approximately £7,800) in compensation. In addition the Court considered it was reasonable, given the absence of other remedies, for the applicant to have sought some public recognition of the breach of his privacy and some vindication of his position before the media commissions and awarded him a further 3,000 Euros (approximately £2,000) towards his costs in making those complaints: (2003) 36 EHRR 41, [128]. The absence of Article 13 from the Convention rights given effect to by the HRA may still present difficulties for a claimant seeking to take this course of action.   **13.144**

14

PROTECTION OF JOURNALISTIC MATERIAL

B. Protection of Sources: the Common Law

(3) The Impact of Norwich Pharmacal

n34 *Ashworth Hospital Authority v Mirror Group Newspapers Ltd* in the House of   **14.09**
Lords is now reported at [2002] 1 WLR 2033.

D. Section 10, Contempt of Court Act 1981

(3) Burden of Proof

n65 Since the decision of the Court of Appeal in *Mersey Care NHS Trust v Ackroyd*   **14.19**

[2003] FSR 820, it is now less likely that a s 10 disclosure order will be made without a full trial. See on this point the Supplement to para 14.29 below.

(4) Necessity

14.25   n75 *Ashworth Hospital Authority v Mirror Group Newspapers Ltd* in the House of Lords is now reported at [2002] 1 WLR 2033.

14.29   Since the decision of the Court of Appeal in *Mersey Care NHS Trust v Ackroyd* [2003] FSR 820, it is now likely to be rare for a s 10 disclosure order to be made without a trial. There was a trial in *Ashworth* itself (see Main Work para 14.24 n74), but not in *Interbrew SA v Financial Times Ltd* (see Main Work para 14.09 n34), where the Court was prepared to make findings, or at least assumptions, about disputed or uncertain issues of fact. In *Mersey Care*, May and Ward LJJ were distinctly reluctant to make a disclosure order without a full trial. May LJ stated at [70]: 'It would be an exceptional case indeed if a journalist were ordered to disclose the identity of his source without the facts of his case being fully examined. I do not say that literally every journalist against whom an order for source disclosure is sought should be entitled to a trial. But the nature of the subject matter argues in favour of a trial in most cases.' Ward LJ agreed, observing at [88] that '. . . to find that a prima facie case for the non-disclosure of a genuine journalist's source of information is displaced without a full investigation into all the facts leaves me feeling uncomfortable'.

(6) The Prevention of Disorder or Crime

14.34   n100 *Ashworth Hospital Authority v Mirror Group Newspapers Ltd* in the House of Lords is now reported at [2002] 1 WLR 2033.

(7) Necessity in the Interests of Justice

14.40   n118 *Ashworth Hospital Authority v Mirror Group Newspapers Ltd* in the House of Lords is now reported at [2002] 1 WLR 2033.

(8) European Developments

14.41   The General Rapporteur on the Media, appointed by the Committee on Culture, Science and Education of the Council of Europe (Doc 9640, 14 January 2003), complained that 'in certain Western European countries, courts still continue to violate the right of journalists to protect their sources of information, and this despite the case-law of the European Court of Human Rights'. She referred in her country by country review to the case of *Interbrew SA v Financial Times Ltd* [2002] EMLR 446, CA, but it is unclear whether she regarded that decision as an instance of a violation of the right to protect sources of information, which of course is far from absolute.

The European Court of Human Rights delivered judgment on 25 February 2003 in the case of *Roemen and Schmit v Luxembourg* (Application no 51772/99). The applicants were a journalist and his lawyer whose premises were subjected to police searches designed to discover the source of a civil service leak about a fine imposed on a Minister for non-payment of tax. In finding a breach of Article 10 in the case of the journalist, and of Article 8 in the case of his lawyer, the Court stated at [57] that it regarded a search aimed at discovering the identity of a journalist's source, even if unproductive, as even more serious than court orders for disclosure of the kind made in *Goodwin v UK* (Application no 17488/90, (1996) EHRR 123). See further the Supplement to para 2.31 above.

(10) Public Interest in the Protection of Sources

In *Mersey Care NHS Trust v Ackroyd* [2003] FSR 820, the successor case to **14.47** *Ashworth* (having obtained the name of the journalist's intermediary from MGN in *Ashworth*, the hospital then attempted to find out from the intermediary, a freelance journalist, the name of the source within the hospital), May LJ referred at [25], [66] to Laws LJ's statement of principle in *Ashworth*, which he set out in full, as 'focal'.

n138 *Ashworth Hospital Authority v Mirror Group Newspapers Ltd* in the House of Lords is now reported at [2002] 1 WLR 2033.

E. Access to Journalists' Sources: Statutory Powers

(1) Police and Criminal Evidence Act 1984

(b) Section 9

(i) Access conditions

n165 See also PACE Code of Practice B, effective as of March 2003, which un- **14.59** derlines the need for specificity in applications for a warrant and requires that any search under Schedule 1 be carried out by an officer of at least the rank of inspector.

n171 In *R v Ipswich Crown Court Ex p NTL Ltd* [2002] 3 WLR 1173 a challenge **14.60** was made to an order for access to special procedure material, namely e-mails automatically stored on NTL's computer system, on the grounds that compliance would involve NTL committing an offence under RIPA 2000, s 1, which makes it an offence for a person intentionally and without lawful authority to intercept any communication in the course of its transmission. The CA upheld the order, holding that it was impossible to accept that it was the intention of Parliament by s 1, RIPA to defeat the powers of police under s 9, PACE for all practical purposes.

(iii) Access conditions: second set

14.64   n177 See also the judgment of the European Court of Human Rights in *Roemen and Schmit v Luxembourg* (25 February 2003, Application no 51772/99) and the Supplement to paras 2.31 and 14.41 above.

(2) Terrorism Act 2000

(a) Duty to supply information to the police

14.68   n188 Under s 38B, inserted by s 117 of the Anti-Terrorism, Crime and Security Act 2001, the Terrorism Act has been amended to add a further criminal offence, of failing without reasonable excuse to disclose information which a person knows or believes might be of material assistance in preventing an act of terrorism or in securing the apprehension, prosecution, or conviction of a person for terrorist acts. Unlike the offence under s 19 Terrorism Act, this new offence is not limited to information obtained in the course of employment.

(5) The Regulation of Investigatory Powers Act 2000

(b) Disclosure of communications data

14.88–14.91   The provisions of RIPA concerning the disclosure of communications data described in these paragraphs (ss 21–25) are not yet in force, with the limited exception of s 21(4) which came into force on 2 October 2000 for the purpose of giving effect to the definition of 'related communications data' in s 20. It should be noted that until the provisions come into force applications for disclosure of communications data would need to be made under ss 9 and 14 and Schedule 1 of PACE, which impose stricter criteria than RIPA.

(e) Confidential journalistic material

14.108   n248 The RIPA codes are now found at www.homeoffice.gov.uk/crimpol/crim-reduc/regulation/codeofpractice/surveillance/index.html.

(f) Non-confidential journalistic information

14.111   n251 See also the judgment of the European Court of Human Rights in *Roemen and Schmit v Luxembourg* (Application no 51772/99, judgment of 25 February 2003) and the Supplement to paras 2.31 and 14.41 above.

(7) Financial Services Act 1986 and Financial Services and Markets Act 2000

(a) Financial Services Act 1986

14.118–14.119   The whole of the Financial Services Act 1986 was repealed by SI 2001/3649, art 3(1)(c), with effect from 1 December 2001.

INDEX